P9-DUR-044

REVISION DECISIONS

Talking Through Sentences and Beyond

Jeff Anderson

&

Deborah Dean

Stenhouse Publishers
Portland, Maine

Stenhouse Publishers
www.stenhouse.com

Copyright © 2014 by Jeff Anderson and Deborah Dean

All rights reserved. Except for the pages in the appendix, which may be photocopied for classroom use, no part of this publication may be reproduced or transmitted in any form or by any means, electronic or mechanical, including photocopy, or any information storage and retrieval system, without permission from the publisher.

Every effort has been made to contact copyright holders and students for permission to reproduce borrowed material. We regret any oversights that may have occurred and will be pleased to rectify them in subsequent reprints of the work.

Library of Congress Cataloging-in-Publication Data
Anderson, Jeff, 1966–
    Revision decisions : talking through sentences and beyond / Jeff Anderson, Deborah Dean.
        pages cm
        ISBN 978-1-62531-006-4 (paperback)—ISBN 978-1-62531-028-6 (ebook)
1. English language—Sentences—Study and teaching (Elementary) 2. English language—Composition and exercises—Study and teaching (Elementary) 3. English language—Sentences—Study and teaching (Secondary) 4. English language—Composition and exercises—Study and teaching (Secondary) I. Dean, Deborah, 1952– II. Title.
        LB1576.A544 2014
        372.62'3044—dc23
                                                                        2014017931

Cover design, interior design, and typesetting by Martha Drury

Manufactured in the United States of America

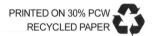
PRINTED ON 30% PCW
RECYCLED PAPER

20 19 18 17 16 15 14   9 8 7 6 5 4 3 2 1

For Terry and David

Your encouragement and willingness to share time with "the writing" make us happy writers.

CONTENTS

Acknowledgments

ACKNOWLEDGMENTS

First we want to thank all the educators whose shoulders we stand on. Neither of us would know about sentence combining if it weren't for the pioneering work of William "Bill" Strong. We are also both indebted to Harry Noden for his fresh look at grammar as a vehicle to support writer's craft in accessible ways. In addition, we are given pause by the talent, enthusiasm, and dedication we see in classrooms across the nation. We especially thank Joseph Wiederhold (Provo High School, Provo, Utah) for trying out lessons in his classroom and literacy coach Alexa Camacho Spahr and teacher Ondria Gadd (Ereckson Middle School, Allen, Texas) for their experimentation with early drafts.

We thank Stenhouse Publishers for all the hard work they put into supporting this project from infancy to now. Three years passes very quickly. Thanks, Bill, Chandra, Chris, Jay, Erin, and our beloved designer, Martha.

Debbie thanks Chris Crowe, Karen Brown, and 2011 summer fellows from the Central Utah Writing Project for their invaluable feedback on and interest in early drafts.

Jeff thanks Terry Thompson for constantly reading and giving feedback and ideas along the way. Thank you for sharing your editing gift and life with me.

PART 1

The Basics

We know that grammar instruction that works includes teaching students strategies for revising and editing, providing targeted lessons on problems that students immediately apply to their own writing, and having students play with sentences like Legos, combining basic sentences into more complex ones.

—Michelle Navarre Cleary

For a seed to achieve its greatest expression, it must come completely undone. The shell cracks, its insides come out and everything changes. To someone who doesn't understand growth, it would look like complete destruction.

—Cynthia Occelli

1

REVISION DECISIONS ARE POSSIBLE

Actively Processing to Develop Options for Revision

To achieve an effective style, [a] writer needs . . . three . . . things: enough mastery of sentence structure to imagine a range of options for expressing an idea, enough understanding of the rhetorical context to predict a sentence's impact on readers, and enough commitment to the idea itself to keep testing options until the sentence says just what it should.

—Nora Bacon

When students talk about their ideas for writing, they often exhibit spark, personality, and pizzazz, expressing interesting ideas fearlessly and creatively. Yet the writing they submit lacks this same enthusiasm and originality. They have the ideas, but what happens between that talk and the written draft?

The space between ideas and words making it to paper is part of the problem. Worrying about how to structure and organize ideas—What comes first? What's the best way to say this?—can stifle students. They sit at the edge of writing, pens hanging over paper, waiting for the perfect words to come before they commit anything—at all—to print.

But once they do commit, they commit. This is another part of the problem: the likelihood of students revising at the sentence level—even once—is right up there with the frequency with which men put down the toilet seat. It isn't happening.

What can we as teachers do to smooth the space between ideas and drafting?

And once words are down on paper, what can teachers do to address this overcommitment to first words as the *only* words? How do we quell the fear of revision? How do we support writers in making decisions about their first words?

Great writing doesn't always happen on our first attempt—nor should we expect it to—if we truly believe in the writing process. Students need options for how to say what they want to say. They need options for revising at the sentence level. Lots of options. They need to feel free to scratch their ideas down on paper. They need to trust that within the writing process they will revise and edit sentences, eventually creating the writing they see in their minds on the pages in front of them. And yes, by this very act of revising, they grow as writers, creating stronger first drafts.

But to become fluent writers brimming with possible decisions, students need to take on writing behaviors—especially the flexibility and creativity of revision, recasting and reordering, deleting and expanding, deciding and evaluating. As teachers, we orchestrate situations that cause talk and problem solving. We create an environment where tussling and playing with words is routine rather than rare. Through interaction and conversation, we create flexible writers who can easily deal with today's changing writing landscape and can also be imprinted with the unchangeable truths about writing and how we compose. To this end, in this book we build upon a teaching method that creates an environment for talk and for making decisions about revision. It's in this messy decision making, in these multiple attempts at meaning, that revisers are born.

True writers revise.

STANDING ON THE SHOULDERS OF SENTENCE COMBINING

Sentence combining, at its simplest, is just what it says: combining sentences. But the point of combining is not simply to put two sentences together (one sentence . . . and . . . another sentence) to make a long sentence. The point of sentence combining is for young writers to see relationships among ideas and to discover more effective ways to show these relationships. So, although at first glance it may look like an exercise in creating long sentences from short ones, sentence combining is really about building relationships among ideas and showing them in clear and interesting ways. Sentence combining shows young writers options for creating effective writing that sings while they gain experience and stamina for relentless revision.

Sentence combining isn't about saying long sentences are better than short sentences, and it isn't about trying to make sentences convoluted. Sentence combining is about playing with ideas and shaping them into effective syntactical patterns that make sense for individual writing situations: sometimes long, sometimes short. *Syntax* is the flow of language—the order and the way in which we combine words. Sentence combining gives students the flexibility of options, revision fluency, and confidence.

SENTENCE COMBINING IN THE PAST

Sentence combining's past is a bit complex, but we'll nail down the big ideas. In the 1970s and early 1980s, sentence combining was in its heyday. Research showed that the practice of combining sentences improved student writing (Braddock, Lloyd-Jones, and Schoer 1963). Period. But in the late 1980s and 1990s, sentence combining was swept out rather quickly with the chalk dust, considered a practice gone by, even though the research continued to support it (Graham and Perin 2007; Myhill 2005).

The demise of sentence combining happened so fast that many believed its passing must have been caused by its ineffectiveness. But research into effective writing instruction, then and now, shows that it does improve student writing. So what happened? According to Connors (2000), sentence combining failed for many reasons. The focus of research changed when, despite the results, no one could explain why sentence combining improved students' writing abilities. In addition, there was an emphasis on writing process, and resistance to anything that focused on the sentence level was seen as anathema to the process movement. So why do we bring it up again in this book, decades later? Why do we, as writing-process believers, hope to reignite the conversation?

Because sentence combining works.

Looking back at sentence combining's past, we can identify teaching practices that happened or didn't happen that contributed to ineffective use: misinterpretations caused by lack of teacher scaffolding, questionable implementation with missing connections, even overscaffolding. All this can be avoided in current instruction with a solid foundation in the writing process and by keeping a few principles in mind.

In its former practice, some teachers tried the examples they were shown in a workshop in their own classrooms. The practice ended there. Sentence combining bore no connection to the actual writing and revision students were doing. Other teachers used sentence-combining workbooks, asking students to combine random sentences that had no context, no process, no inquiry, and no connections beyond the activity. The sentences students created were "corrected" in terms of how close they came to the original. There was little evaluative talk about how the structures students created worked or didn't work, little reflection on the effectiveness of sentences, little practical application to students' writing. In many classes, writing was still about being right or wrong, not about the deep thinking involved in the many attempts and approximations. We want to enhance the research-proven strategy of sentence combining and all the thinking and flexibility that come along with it.

THE FUTURE: REVISION DECISIONS

We include scaffolding in this book with the appropriate emphasis on the key principles that will enhance success, including context and conversation that centers on revision. First, semantics matter. Note that in this book we've shifted the focus from the idea of simply combining sentences to the decisions we make about revision. The shift more appropriately addresses what twenty-first-century writers need: to be flexible in their thinking and resilient in considering options. A revision decision is actually more descriptive of the strategy's twenty-first-century value and allure. Revision is where writers get their wings, their flexibility, their effectiveness.

Revision of sentences is today's solution to a first-draft society that is obsessed with brief communication and information. Everything is done instantly and without much revision. Write. Hit "send" or "post" or "tweet." Revising early and revising often is one way to put the brakes on the runaway speed of writing that compels young writers to skip reflection and rereading, treating these activities as obsolete as last year's gadget. Revision decisions slow writers down to consider meaning and their options for shaping and connecting ideas.

Writing Next (Graham and Perin 2007) clearly points us toward sentence combining as one of the eleven research-proven methods highlighted to effectively develop writers in grades four through twelve. That recommendation matches with what we know about brain and fluency research (Eagleman 2011; Gladwell 2011): students learn best when actively processing information and when practicing what we actually want them to be able to do. This book will show you how to activate revision with your students while developing patterns and practices that will benefit them in other stages of the writing process, including later initial drafts and larger revision decisions.

REVISION DECISIONS IN ACTION

Before we share some of the principles that help a revision-decision lesson work, let's look at them at play in a seventh-grade classroom working with an excerpt from Albert Marrin's *Black Gold: The Story of Oil in Our Lives* (2012). We love using published sentences from interesting, effective writing. First, we unrevise, undoing the revision work of crafting, combining, and connecting ideas, so young writers can follow in the footsteps of a professional author's revision decisions.

I display the following sentences, which are derived by uncombining one of Marrin's sentences and separating its content into four simple sentences.

You need to understand oil.
We must begin with the key rule.
This is a key rule of science.
Change alone is changeless.

"Every time we see sentences chunked together like this," I say, pointing to the chunk or cluster of sentences, "they are primed for revision. Our goal is to take these four sentences and see if we can say the same thing with fewer words—maybe even in just one sentence. I'll show you how to begin with the first two sentences. That's how the sentence-revision process starts."

To understand oil we must begin with the key rule.

"When I look at the new sentence we've combined," I say, "I think we need a comma. Where would y'all put a comma?"

"Well, when you said it, you paused after *oil*," a student offers.

"That makes sense. A chunk of the sentence is *to understand oil*. To set this introductory information—or infinitive phrase—off, I use a comma."

To understand oil, we must begin with the key rule.

"Okay, now let's see if we can pull the third sentence into this sentence." I reread it. "Any ideas? One of our options when combining is to *delete* words or phrases. Is there a place where we can delete some repeated words or words that aren't doing any work?"

"This sentence is just saying that the key rule is *of science*," Marissa says. "It doesn't really say anything else new."

"So," I say, "what if we just take what we already have and say, *To understand oil, we must begin with the science key rule* or *a key rule for science*? Or *is* there another way to say it? How about this?"

I revise on the board:

To understand oil, we must begin with the key rule of science.

"I wonder if we can make one sentence with all these sentences. But how can I put the sentence *Change alone is changeless* into our sentence? We've already taken it from four sentences down to two. And that would be acceptable, but because the four sentences were clustered together, we know there could be a way to make it into one sentence. We are going to challenge ourselves as writers to find a way. *Talk it out* with your group and see if you can meet the revision challenge. We always talk out our sentences first, trying to make the best sense we can."

Turning it over to the students won't necessarily produce a workable sentence, but it initiates the conversation, the active processing, the flexing and shaping, the revising and deciding. More than likely, they will come up with a few ways as this class of seventh graders did.

"Make it a compound sentence," one group suggests:

To understand oil, we must begin with the key rule of science, and the key rule is change alone is changeless.

This response shows that students see the connection between the sentences—they understand the meaning. At this point, I am broadly evaluating. I don't want to rain on their sentence parade by saying "Repetitive." I celebrate the fact that they see the connection and use a grammatical structure that makes sense. Options. Flexibility.

Another group offers something different:

To understand oil, we must begin with a key rule of science, change alone is changeless.

"We are doing that 'a position' thing," Brad says.

"Oh, the appositive or *apposition*," I say. I facilitate the students' connecting to prior learning on appositives. Last week, we'd discussed how useful appositives were. A grammatical structure that packs information into one sentence. I celebrate the application of what we notice in our reading and writing. We rename and/or expand on a noun—in this case, *science*.

"Yeah, the rule of science is the same thing, so it's renaming the rule as the rule," Charmayne says.

"One thing we will do this year is compare and contrast how an author put together the same cluster of sentences," I say. "Do you want to see how Albert Marrin revised these sentences?" I display Marrin's sentence from *Black Gold*:

> *To understand oil, we must begin with the key rule of science: change alone is changeless.*

I hear a gasp when students see the unthought-of colon. Another option is presented, noted, and perhaps used later. Students talk with their tablemates about what they notice about how Marrin combined the sentences:

- What did the author do that was similar to our revision?
- What was different?
- Why do you think the author made similar/different choices?

And now we have a new option: the colon. This is a perfect time to add some instruction to students' noticings. So much natural learning and decision making is possible while revising sentences. We talked through just one sentence, and already we are becoming more deft and flexible at sentence acrobatics.

When we start slow and small, we actually accelerate learning, stumbling on possibilities. It's not about learning another rule such as how to use colons; it's about writers discovering another option to make their writing strong. Possibilities.

PRINCIPLES FOR MAKING REVISION DECISIONS

A major drawback of sentence combining in the past was that it was seen as more of a grammar activity than a revision activity. It's actually grammar *through* revision. The following principles mark effective use of revision at the sentence level to improve writing overall, at both drafting and revising stages. The revision process gives us another chance to resee, reformulate, redesign. We integrate revision decisions within effective practice of the writing process, the study of models, inquiry, and collaboration—all research-based, best-composition practices identified in *Writing Next* (Graham and Perin 2007). We know from experience that when we implement these practices effectively, students are better writers, readers, and thinkers.

Throughout this book, these key principles of revision will enhance its integration into writing-process classrooms. Having these principles in place is the backbone of an environment where revision decisions happen—a space where risk and skill are supported and sustained:

- Create a Context for Revising Sentences.
- Invite Collaboration That Becomes The Conversation in Writers' Heads.
- Allow Choice, Risk-Taking, and Error.
- Make Meaning by Reflecting and Evaluating.

Principle 1: Create a Context for Revising Sentences

Students need to be writing all the time, constantly generating ideas for drafting, revising, or polishing. They should experience writing at all stages of the writing process, and even, as writers at all levels of development do, have some pieces of writing that don't go anywhere, that stay drafts forever, beginnings without endings. When writers compose and revise writing regularly and often, they come to see the writing process as inherent to their work, not simply something they "do" (or fake) for English class.

Research—and our own experiences as teachers—shows us that separating grammar and revision instruction from writing isn't effective (Anderson 2005, 2007, 2011; Dean 2010; and Myhill 2005). Instead, students need to have supportive instruction that they can apply to their ongoing writing.

In these lessons, we give students experience with doing this revision—practice with rethinking and reseeing. The writing process often breaks down at the revision stage because students haven't tussled with recasting sentences enough, and haven't had multiple opportunities to see phrases and clauses added or moved.

Until students have practiced rethinking and revising their writing, they can't reach that point skilled writers achieve where thought is revised and structures are unconsciously called upon and used. After we work with students and sentences in this way, we find our own initial drafts richer for the possibilities we've learned through revising sentences. Yagoda says it this way: "[Style] emerges when writers are comfortable with their tools" (2004, B16).

How do writers get comfortable with the tools of words and sentences? How do we get our students started in doing what writers do to revise on a more automatic and regular basis? How do we help them see the options and get the practice that fluency requires (Gladwell 2011)? By playing with ideas and sentences. Here's a short example of what that looks like in a classroom.

In a fifth-grade classroom, I display a compound sentence:

Many large animals are dangerous, but smaller animals can be dangerous too.

We read the sentence aloud. "The writing strategy writers use more than any other is revising," I say. "What are some ways we could resee this sentence?"

"We could add more detail," Destiny says.

"Let's do that. What are some large animals we know are dangerous?"

"Elephants!"

"Yeah, those are big, and tigers; they rip people to shreds!" Adam says.

"Let's put that in a sentence," I say. I write the following:

It's easy to see that elephants and tigers are dangerous because they are so big.

"What I am noticing," I say, standing back and looking at the students' sentence, displayed beneath the original, "is that there are endless ways writers can say something. They have many options. Writers keep rereading and trying things out until they find what works the best. First, we always talk the new ideas through, making sense. You discovered that adding detail could help. Once we added detail, there was another way to say what we wanted to say. Let's look at how Steve Jenkins [2009a] writes a similar idea about animals in *Never Smile at a Monkey*":

Everyone knows that tigers, crocodiles, sharks, and other large predators are dangerous. Many smaller animals are also well-known threats. People do their best to avoid rattlesnakes, black widow spiders, and piranhas, to name just a few.

"He added different details," Carlos says.

"Yep," I say. "He added details like you, yet he said it in another way." I look out at the students. "The point is that we pause after we've written something. We evaluate it. Writers aren't always satisfied with how everything comes out the first time. They try to rework or revise sentences. That's one of the most important writing strategies we will learn this year. When we play with sentences and try new things, it makes our rhetorical muscles grow, meaning we can say stuff more clearly, and our writing gets better and better.

"Now let's go back to what we wrote in our notebooks yesterday. We've already paused. We know it's good to look at our writing after a time. Now let's reread your writing a couple of times and see if you can play with any of your sentences. Consider adding details like Jenkins did. We'll share some revisions in a bit." We are creating a need for options of multiple ways to say whatever we have to say. That is a context in and of itself.

A final point about classroom context: the thinking that occurs within sentence play should find its way, eventually, to students' writing. When students write, particularly polished pieces of writing, they apply the concepts they have learned during sentence revision. Young writers develop an ability to explain why they applied the concept as they did. The explanation doesn't need to be exhaustive, but it's important that this kind of thinking happens consistently.

Another aspect of context has to do with the sentences themselves. Sentences don't usually exist alone in many places, though that's changing. (Think, for example, about advertisements, Twitter, or Facebook status updates.) Much of the time, what makes a sentence effective is how it fits with the sentences around it. It may be a short sentence next to a long one, or an element of a sentence that is repeated. It may even be a surprising twist from what readers expected. Whatever the specifics, sentences connect meaningfully to the sentences that come before and after them. It's important for students to see a context and how it matters to sentence construction and overall sentence flow. In fact, Schuster (2005) says it's *dangerous* to ignore context when we study sentences for style. We encourage students ultimately to work with paragraphs, not only single sentences, as paragraphs provide another, more extensive context.

Ideally, teachers create sentence sets from the texts their students are reading. That provides the best context. If the sentences we decombine don't come from a text students are reading, we contextualize the revising of sentences with a short book talk about how the passage we are working with fits into it. In this way, we interest students in reading the text, too. Again, context matters so that students have a sense of sentences existing as part of a larger unit.

Principle 2: Invite Collaboration That Becomes The Conversation in Writers' Heads

When students have four short sentences, they begin talking out how to put the ideas together—*deleting* a repeated word here, starting and restarting. Then, perhaps they *form new verb endings*, using collaboration and conversation to see if the meaning and sense are effective. Another student piggybacks on one student's attempt, improving it or not. Each talked-out attempt is evaluated, validated, and revised, kept or rejected.

James Britton is known for saying, "Reading and writing float on a sea of talk" (1993), and the research about talk and active processing continue through Marzano, Pickering, and Pollock (2007); Graham and Perin (2007); and Langer et al. (2000). Revision of sentences most certainly sinks without talk. It is in the essential conversation, in the starts and restarts, in the tentativeness of speech, in the richness of syntactic background already imprinted in students' minds, in the risk-free possibilities that talk allows for that we find the true benefits of revision decisions. This is where the transformation happens. It is in talking out sentences and our innate desire for things to make sense that students find their style, their voice, their flexibility.

One way we can help students use this talk so it will transfer to their writing is through the discussion of choices. When students, either alone or in groups, revise a cluster of sentences in more than one way, they select one as their "favorite." It's important that they attempt to articulate why they selected one sentence over another. Considering the rationale behind the choice is an essential element contributing to growth from revision; without it, the revision learning stays at the exercise. The talk in class helps writers begin to develop a rationale or purpose behind their writing choices, which bolsters understanding of author's purpose, an important step in their development.

One aspect that might contribute to the difficulty in articulating effects is that students don't have a vocabulary for those effects. To support student talk, teachers can model by explaining their choices, including these Three *Es* of Effective Sentences, which help writers evaluate a specific construction:

- *Economy*: Like being careful with money, being efficient with language can be a good reason for choosing a particular sentence over another version. Writers delete for economy.
- *Emphasis*: Writers create a variety of structures that result in a variety of effects through rearranging. Words in certain places can get more attention than words in other places—so choosing certain words to go in those attention-getting (or attention-losing) spots can make a different idea stand out.
- *Effect*: Some syntactical choices help to create a tone, fitting somewhere on a range from simplicity to sophistication. For example, syntactical construction might seem so common that it creates a pedestrian tone, as in this example from Schuster (2005): *My dog and I hunt, fish, walk, eat, and sleep together.* Or this more sophisticated construction: *My dog and I do everything together. Hunt, fish, walk, eat, and sleep together.*

Once modeled, the Three *Es* of Effective Sentences can continue as part of collaborative talk that works its way into student thought—even at the drafting stage.

Principle 3: Allow Choice, Risk-Taking, and Error

When students have open choice in how to revise sentences, you never know what they might do. This choice is essential to play and to learning. It is also essential to their developing as writers. However, being flexible in our instruction makes some teachers nervous about embracing uncertainty:

- There isn't an answer key?
- Who knows what students will do when they have options?
- What if they come up with a structure I can't name?
- What if they can't combine in any other way besides adding *and*?
- What if they make run-on sentences and open up new problems?
- What if . . . ?

And it's all A-OK. The point is flexibility. We are trying things out, experimenting and discovering. Learning—for students and for us—isn't usually a straight road without bumps. Instead, it's often a bumpy, winding road with some potholes. We don't speed along it, but it gets us where we need to be.

If students do compose something and teachers don't know how, in that moment, to respond, there's nothing wrong with saying, "That's an interesting construction. Can you write the sentence on another piece of paper and leave it with me to study?" Students won't be bothered at all. Although in this book we provide some direction for how we have done this revision work with our students, we hope you will adapt our general ideas to whatever your students do and to whatever they need in the moment.

Another aspect of flexibility occurs when students apply their learning to their writing. Consistent engagement with revising sentences will produce effects, but what individual students learn may vary and will depend on readiness as well as other factors. We can *and should* expect students to apply what they learn in their polished writing, but we also need to remember that this learning won't happen overnight. Students' experimentation may lead to some less effective sentence choices before it leads to more effective ones—much like learning something new usually does.

And students need to be flexible—as thinkers and writers. When we give them sentences to consider, we ask them to revise each cluster of sentences in at least two ways. By doing that, we encourage them to stretch, to move past their first choice and attempt something they might not otherwise consider. This risk taking gives them a chance to truly play and perhaps to fail, but perhaps to discover something even better and freer. After they revise in multiple ways, they select the best combination of words and prepare to explain why it is the best. Evaluation. This practice not only develops flexible thinking about writing but also prepares students to be able to analyze and reflect on the choices they make as writers—all key elements in their development as readers and writers.

Principle 4: Make Meaning by Reflecting and Evaluating

The brain seeks to make meaning. It can't help itself. Revision is all about meaning making and making sense. It's about looking closely at words, attempting to create clear and concise and connected meaning. Making revision decisions requires writers to pay attention—close attention. And part of paying attention is talk. David Eagleman (2011), a neurologist and author, argues that the way we bring ideas to our conscious level of attention is to have a conversation about them. This active processing is the very thing revisers need to make their writing effective.

Reflective conversations and evaluative talk increase the possibilities for transfer of that thinking. In *Because Writing Matters*, Carl Nagin (2006) addresses this important aspect of learning to write: "To develop as writers, students also need the opportunity to articulate their own awareness and understanding of their processes in learning to write. Research has shown the importance of such metacognitive thinking in becoming a better writer" (82).

Getting students to think reflectively is not easy. It's some of the hardest work we do. In some ways, students become almost trained to think of each activity, exercise, writing task, and strategy practice as an entity unto itself. They forget that learning lasts. Initial attempts at reflection can be discouraging.

To counter this, we ask students to do hard thinking about sentences and meaning and style. Now we want them to move that thinking toward some kind of future action where it might be useful. This kind of thinking isn't easy, but it's essential for their development as writers and thinkers. We can help in this development by modeling the ways in which reflection guides our development as writers. Begin with oral reflection in class. Model reflective thought, and then invite students who understand this reflective thinking to share. As students develop the ability to reflect, the potential for transfer increases, and we are more likely to see students applying the thinking in a variety of situations.

REVISION IS PLAYING WITH SENTENCES

Overall, revision decisions require an element of play. Yes, play—freedom, exploration, discovery. Play is an integral part of what helps revision discussions develop writers and foster the critical thinking and flexibility essential to learning about language. In play, we take risks—and we are comfortable taking them. We are free to make mistakes and discover what works best through trial and error. We try something to see how it works, and if need be, we change it to suit our needs better. Think of putting a puzzle together. Even when there is a spot for every piece, we still try the pieces in multiple places, in places where they clearly don't fit and in places where they could. We laugh when a piece doesn't fit—and then we try it somewhere else. No one slaps our hands or questions our ability to meet puzzle-putting-together standards. The same is true of play with language.

Play with language involves trying and imagining and then trying again. In the lessons that follow, we revise sentences and paragraphs, and in so doing, encourage students to find what makes the writing process work: thinking, rethinking, analyzing, and asking questions.

What follows is not, of course, a one-size-fits-all process. We encourage teachers and students to think about revision in a new way with the sentences and paragraphs we read and write. It's sentence, paragraph, and style play that's engaging, enlightening, and energizing.

But revision decisions are more than grammar and writing and reading.

They're more than writing process.

They're more than grammar and style.

And they're more—definitely more—than combining sentences.

2

THE VOCABULARY OF REVISION DECISIONS

Introducing DRAFT with a Five-Day Lesson Plan

Let's say it's a mess. But you have a chance to fix it. You try to be clearer. Or deeper. Or more eloquent.

—Susan Sontag

Writing is a series of attempts that is often messy—drafting, revising. Many things are tried; some will be fixed, some discarded, and others memorialized in print, making it the best it can be—for now. It isn't permanent—at least not until the writer says so. And it isn't often that we stop after the first try. It's like shooting hoops: a series of throws until the ball swooshes through the net. That is the very heart of revision. Yet it's far too common for young writers to see revision like they see editing. In editing, we correct a few things, and then we're good. Revision needs to have a sense that a window of possibility is still open to allow another draft in. Students need to know that it is in the reshaping and retweaking—in the redrafting—that we find what's clearer, deeper, and more eloquent. In revision, we find, to paraphrase Samuel Taylor Coleridge, "the best words and the best order" and turn mere words into poetry.

Sentences are a writer's tool, and their positioning demonstrates relationships in the way that best fits our mood and message. We want students to know that writers revise sentences. And it's in this revising that the ever-onward-and-upward spiral of a writer's growth commences.

To get writers started in the process, we break down the essential actions for revising and combining and recasting our ideas. Mnemonics are a starting point, not an end point, but often the concreteness, the anchor, and the ease that mnemonics provide give us basic confidence and competence when attacking a new endeavor. Our mnemonic anchor for revision decisions is D-R-A-F-T: not only does DRAFT signal writers about the actions they can take, but the word *draft* itself reminds them of the freedom of revision:

> **D**elete unnecessary and repeated words.
> **R**earrange sentence parts/chunks.
> **A**dd connectors.
> **F**orm new verb endings.
> **T**alk it out.

Since a common language aids in making revision-decision conversations work, we begin with a set of lessons to teach the DRAFT strategies, which will launch language and action for all the revision lessons that follow. This vocabulary will expand as we return to these important shaping actions again and again. Young authors need concrete actions to take, not endless edicts to "revise." They can't revise when they don't know what to do.

Here is a five-day lesson plan to introduce writers to the DRAFT mnemonic and the actions revisers do. And, as we always try to do in this book, there are a few pointers along the way.

WHAT DO SENTENCE REVISERS DO?

The first act is to delete, to rid our writing of the extraneous. We start here with replicable actions revisers can do.

Day One: Delete

It's important to scrutinize every word, phrase, and clause—to see whether you can cut it to give you a sentence that conveys the same meaning more swiftly.
—Bruce Larson, *Stunning Sentences*

When we first write, getting our ideas down is paramount. As we look again at our writing, we look for ways to hone our message. Sometimes we add to what we've written, but we also have a friend in the delete key. Deleting is key to revising sentences.

Repetition. Words that don't do any work. These are what deleters hunt for and scrub from their writing. We love our first words, but the only way to keep our love of them pure is to make sure we use only the ones that are needed and best get our message across.

To introduce the idea to young writers, I tell them the story of my ever-messy room as a kid. "My mom was always telling me to clean up my room," I say.

Students smile and nod.

"She'd want me to pick up my clothes off the floor and get rid of the things that didn't fit or didn't belong in my room. Writing is like a room."

When appropriate, I make the following points throughout the lesson. When we start the writing process, our goal is to get our ideas down on paper, all of them. Sometimes we start in one direction and then discover another. Once we know what we want to say, we look back at our writing and make sure there isn't anything that doesn't fit anymore. Is there anything that can be thrown away? Writing that is clear and orderly is easier for our readers. If we have a lot of extra words that are repetitive or empty, it's harder for our readers to make meaning.

I explain that one of the most useful revision decisions a writer makes is choosing what stays in the writing and what doesn't. Because what's left becomes more important after we've cleared the "clothes off the floor," we help our readers navigate through our writing without tripping.

I read an effective passage from the opening page of Steve Sheinkin's (2012) award-winning *Bomb: The Race to Build—and Steal—the World's Most Dangerous Weapon*:

> *He had a few more minutes to destroy seventeen years of evidence.*
>
> *Still in pajamas, Harry Gold raced around his cluttered bedroom, pulling out desk drawers, tossing boxes out of the closet, and yanking books from the shelves. Everywhere he looked were incriminating papers—a plane ticket stub, a secret report, a letter from a fellow spy.*
>
> *Gold ripped the papers into shreds, carried two fistfuls to the bathroom, shoved them into the toilet, and flushed. Then he ran back to his bedroom, grabbed the rest of the pile, and stumbled on slippers down the stairs to the cellar, where he pushed the stuff to the bottom of an overflowing garbage can.*
>
> *The doorbell rang.*

"What do you notice?"

The class responds that it's exciting, and they want to know more.

"Do you think this is his first draft?" I ask.

Of course they don't, but it's worth it to have *them* say it.

"Writers actually draft even after they draft," I say. "They try some passages, some sentences, over and over again to get them just right."

I show students a first draft the writer could have written.

He had only a few more precious minutes to quickly get rid of seventeen years of incriminating evidence.

"To keep writing moving, it can be as simple as getting rid of words that aren't really doing any work." I strike through *only* and *precious*. "I can also delete four words when one will do." I strike through *quickly get rid of* and replace it with *destroy*. "That's part of revision, deleting words that aren't doing any work or that could be more precise."

He had ~~only~~ a few more ~~precious~~ minutes to ~~quickly get rid of~~ destroy seventeen years of ~~incriminating~~ evidence.

"Writers also look for unnecessary repetition," I continue, displaying the next passage:

Harry Gold raced around his cluttered bedroom. He pulled out desk drawers. He tossed boxes out of the closet. He yanked books from the shelves.

"Does anybody see a problem?"

"Repeating," students answer.

"I know we aren't supposed to start a bunch of sentences with the same word," Dwayne says.

"Right. Lists can be a deleter's friend," I say. I draw a line through three uses of the word *he*.

Harry Gold raced around his cluttered bedroom. ~~He~~ pulled out desk drawers. ~~He~~ tossed boxes out of the closet. ~~He~~ yanked books from the shelves.

"At first glance, it's easy to see that we can make a list by adding some commas and an *and*." I rewrite the sentence:

Harry Gold pulled out the desk drawers, tossed boxes out of the closet, and yanked books from the shelves.

"Look at how Steve Sheinkin kept the sense of hurry and desperation by cutting all three *he's* and changing things to help it all make sense," I say.

Harry Gold raced around his cluttered bedroom, pulling out desk drawers, tossing boxes out of the closet, and yanking books from the shelves.

"What did he change?" Ruben asks.
"Good question, Ruben," I say. "Does anyone see the changes?"
"The verbs," Melissa says, squinting. "He changed them."
"Indeed." I point to the verbs *pulling, tossing,* and *yanking.* "He *formed new verb endings*, adding *-ing* to each, making participles. And to show panic even more, Sheinkin added the words *still in pajamas.* How does that show more panic?"

Still in pajamas, Harry Gold raced around his cluttered bedroom, pulling out desk drawers, tossing boxes out of the closet, and yanking books from the shelves.

After that discussion, we note how the *-ing* form of these verbs (participles) shows the flurry of movement. Though our focus is emphasizing the act of deleting, we also frontload the other strategies clandestinely, such as *talking it out.* If young writers aren't reading their sentences aloud, then they should be, so we practice *talking it out* long before we get to the Talk It Out lesson. In addition, Sheinkin also *formed new verb endings* to delete unneeded words. It can't hurt to use the forthcoming language as we move through the process, as more often than not it's a combination of several actions denoted by the letters of the DRAFT mnemonic that we use to revise.

"One thing writers do is delete," I continue. "Now you try deleting like Sheinkin with a partner." Pointing to some chart paper, I say, "His first draft might have looked like this":

Everywhere he looked there were incriminating papers. There was a plane ticket. There was a secret report. In addition, there was a letter from a fellow spy.

Now students try their hand at deleting. We share our newly crafted sentences and see what we deleted, making sure to talk about why we made the decisions we did. Then Sheinkin's version is revealed, not to test for correctness, but to show possibility.

Everywhere he looked were incriminating papers—a plane ticket stub, a secret report, a letter from a fellow spy.

D R A F T

Day Two: Rearrange Words and Chunks

To shift the structure of a sentence alters the meaning of that sentence, as definitely and inflexibly as the position of a camera alters the meaning of the object photographed.

—Joan Didion

"Yesterday we learned that writers revise by deleting unneeded words," I say. "Another nifty tool revisers have is the ability to rearrange words and groups of words, like phrases and clauses. I learned as an adult that it's easier to keep my home neat if I put everything in its place: for example, all the T-shirts in one drawer, jeans in another. Some things belong together. Others belong apart. Sometimes it takes a bit of trial and error, testing and tweaking."

In general, there are ideal places for phrases and clauses to dwell, too; however, only through trying several different ways can we be sure we have them in the optimal order.

Watching a comedy the other night I heard a character say, "I really like Mindy's haircut, despite what everyone else says." That cracked me up. But the character could have quipped, "Despite what everyone else says, I really like Mindy's haircut." Actually both are funny. But which is best, and why? In the end, it's funnier to make Mindy think she's getting a compliment and then hear the opposite, *despite what everyone else says*.

We want kids to see how phrases and clauses and words in different order and placement create different effects.

In class, we return to the Sheinkin passage from *Bomb* to discover the power of rearranging words, phrases, and clauses.

"Let's look at these sentences." I display the passage. "First, are there other ways to say the same thing?"

> Trying to slow his heartbeat, he took a few deep breaths, then opened the door and saw the men he expected: Scott Miller and Richard Brennan, who worked as agents for the FBI.

"I can transpose the opening phrase and clause, or switch places," I say.

> He took a few deep breaths, trying to slow his heartbeat . . .

"Which do you like better?" I ask.

"I like that it's saying what he did first, then why, instead of why before what he did," Lisa says.

"So it makes better sense in that order?"

A few eyes squint to see what Lisa means, so I restate it, pointing out how the action preceded the why.

"Wait," I say. "There's one more thing I can change. Yes, we can move phrases to the front or the back or all around, but sometimes we can do double duty by reordering words in such a way as to delete some. Look here after the colon."

Scott Miller and Richard Brennan, who worked as agents for the FBI.

"What if I move the information in the *who* clause up front, like this?"

FBI agents Scott Miller and Richard Brennan

"Is this better?" I ask.

"Yeah."

"Why?" I ask.

The students sigh, disappointed that I am just going to keep asking questions.

Eventually, we articulate how moving *FBI* in front of *agents* (*FBI agents*) means we can lose the words *who worked as* and *for the* and still say the same thing more economically and thus more effectively.

"So watch," I say. "Is there a word that can be changed into an adjective like *FBI*? Are there words that can be cut?" I display another sentence based on the text of *Bomb.*

The scenes speed around the world, from labs that were secret to raids by commandos to spy meetings on street corners.

"See if you and a partner can find anything to reorder. Talk your options through. Let your ears help you judge which is better. Try more than one thing: something else, anything else." The point is trial and error. Discovery. Flexibility. Evaluation. I emphasize that the secret to revision lies in persistence, trying again and again and again, honing your craft.

After students revise and share, we compare our versions with Sheinkin's published version. Again, it isn't about matching it, but if no one saw this possibility, here it is, and if someone did, they feel as if they've won a prize.

The scenes speed around the world, from secret labs to commando raids to street-corner spy meetings.

"Here's another one to try."

The FBI agents were unconvinced, so they had come to search his house.

"Remember how we just talked about reordering and deleting at the same time?" I ask. "What word here could we put in a different place that would also allow us to delete other words?"

Students give me a long pause, looking at the sentence intently, trying to uncover its secrets. After fifteen seconds of wait time, I help a bit. "If we were using this sentence to describe the FBI agents, is there a word we could use?"

"*Unconvinced!*" shouts Ethan.

"Sure. So we can move *unconvinced* around and take out *were*. What other changes would that make to our sentence?"

"We could say, *The unconvinced FBI agents had come to search his house*," Ethan continues.

"Yes, we could. By moving that one word, we can eliminate other words, so we get a twofer: deleting *and* rearranging! Good work. Here's the sentence in Sheinkin's book:"

Unconvinced, the FBI agents had come to search his house.

"What do you notice about the different order he chose?"

We want to make sure students understand that rearranging is not without hazards, so we show them one more example. "Let's look at this example sentence from the book":

Overwhelmed by exhaustion, he turned to the FBI agents.

"Here we can see that an original idea might have been that Harry was overwhelmed by exhaustion, so he turned to the agents," I say. "The writer, deleting words and rearranging words, might create a different sentence, putting the action ahead of the description. What is the different effect of this arrangement?"

He turned to the FBI agents, overwhelmed by exhaustion.

"We still know that it's this guy, Harry, who is exhausted," Mark says, "but someone else might think it's the FBI guys."

"Sure," I say. "So what do we learn from that?"

Students wait for me to answer my own question, but I wait longer. Finally someone breaks the uncomfortable silence.

"Be careful?" Tristan mumbles.

"Tell me more about what you mean, Tristan."

"Well," Tristan sighs, "be careful, because you could be trying to make it better and instead you make it worse."

"We always have to pay attention to what we mean, don't we? Moving phrases and clauses gives different effects and creates different relationships among our ideas; by combining or moving words, changing parts of speech and deleting, we can revise our writing to its trimmest. And there is often an optimal choice. We always have to think about what we are actually saying."

This is the first of many questions we will have about descriptive phrases and clauses being close to what they modify. The closer they are, the better chance we have of being clear.

Day Three: Add Connectors

The writer . . . connects words that slide easily together or ignites the civil war of the phrase.

—Don Murray

Connector words and punctuation are endlessly useful to show relationships *among* and *between* words. From prepositions like *among* and *between* to words that show addition like *which* or even ubiquitous conjunctions like *and* or *but*, we all rely on connector words. (Not to mention how useful *like* was in that sentence.) And it's not only words. Punctuation helps us connect our thoughts as well. We can use it in the following ways:

- Call on a colon to introduce a list (as I just did);
- Situate a semicolon between items in a list that contain commas or other punctuation (as I do here);
- Position parentheses (see above) to clarify—or divide with dashes;
- Connect, separate, and list using commas.

Overall, connectors create cohesion in our prose. Our focus is to tease out the ways we can show relationships within a sentence, clarifying meaning and compressing ideas to their essential core. This can't be done in one lesson, but needs to be shown in many. Here we'll give a broad overview of things that could be addressed. We could spend a week on connectors alone. But what do all these relationships that the connectors show have to do with revising sentences for clarity and concision? Look at the following chart (Figure 2.1) and excerpt to see how Neil Gaiman (2013) uses connector words and punctuation in *Fortunately, the Milk*:

Use Connectors Like Gaiman Does	
Model from *Fortunately, the Milk*	**Function of Connector Words**
There was only orange juice *in* the fridge.	The **preposition** *in* shows where.
Nothing else *that* you could . . .	*That* is a **relative pronoun** *that* connects.
put *on* cereal,	The **preposition** *on* shows where.
unless you think that . . .	*Unless* is a **subordinating conjunction** that contrasts.
ketchup *or* mayonnaise *or* pickle juice would be nice *on* your Toastios,	*Or* is a **coordinating conjunction** that indicates choices.
which I do not,	*Which* is a **relative pronoun** that relates ideas to each other.
and	*And* is a **coordinating conjunction**, which connects equal ideas.
neither did my little sister,	*Neither* is a conjunction that shows agreement between two negative statements.
although she has eaten some pretty weird things in her day,	The **subordinating conjunction** *although* contrasts.
like mushrooms in chocolate.	*Like* is a **preposition** linking an example.

Figure 2.1
If the connector word appeared more than once, we defined only the first occurrence. (Grammarians, please forgive the use of *like* in the title of this figure. We know it should be *as*, but it's so often used, we thought it excusable here.)

There was only orange juice in the fridge. Nothing else that you could put on cereal, unless you think that ketchup or mayonnaise or pickle juice would be nice on your Toastios, which I do not, and neither did my little sister, although she has eaten some pretty weird things in her day, like mushrooms in chocolate.

Prepositions are a basic way to show meaningful relationships among and between words. We'll start our exploration with them.

Prepositions as Connectors

The most basic of connectors, prepositions, help orient a reader in time and space, and introduce examples, contrasts, and comparisons. *Where* are you supposed to put something, or *when* do you need to be there? (And where is *there* for that matter?) Many remember prepositions as everywhere a squirrel can go (*up* a tree, *across* the fence, *in* the potted plants, *under* the birdbath). And that's an excellent start, but prepositions are used to indicate more than mere location. Notice how April Pulley Sayre shows prepositions' potential by precisely placing these connectors in her book *Here Come the Humpbacks!* (2013). (See Figure 2.2.)

			What Do PREPOSITIONS Do?		

What Do PREPOSITIONS Do?

Prepositions show time and place, and introduce examples, contrasts, and comparisons.

Purpose	Examples			Models from *Here Come the Humbacks!* by April Pulley Sayre (2013; bold added)
One Point in Time	*on*	*at*	*in*	**In** every ocean on Earth, humpback whales swim.
Extended Time	*since* *for* *by*	*from* *to* *until*	*during* *with(in)*	Their skin is scarred **from** past competitions.
Direction	*to* *toward*	*on* *onto*	*in* *into*	A boat coasts **toward** the sleepy whales.
Location	*above* *across* *against* *ahead of* *along* *among* *around* *at* *by*	*behind* *below* *beside* *beneath* *between* *from* *in* *inside* *on*	*off* *out of* *over* *near* *through* *toward* *under* *within*	**Through** this cord, her body has fed him for eleven and a half months.
Introduce Examples or Comparisons	*like*	*as* *with*	*for*	Her blue-gray head, bumpy **as** a pickle, lifts and looks.

Figure 2.2
In this chart, the model sentences come from April Pulley Sayre's *Here Come the Humbacks!* (2013).

Conjunctions as Connectors

Like the Schoolhouse Rock cartoon asks, "Conjunction junction, what's your function?" It's true that conjunctions are used to hook up phrases, clauses, and words, *but* there are actually two types of conjunctions (see Figure 2.3). Like all other connectors, conjunctions are basically joiners. They are described here, not so much so you can use these exact words when explaining to students, but to help you discern which parts your students will need clarified so they can apply them well. Our goal is not for students to memorize the labels, but to understand their function in showing the kinds of connections between ideas. See the main points in Figure 2.3.

Relative Pronouns as Connectors

Relative pronouns are a rather useful set of words *that* show relationships between ideas, just as *that* does in the first part of this sentence. (See Figure 2.4 for a list of relative pronouns.) We often use these words without much

What Do CONJUNCTIONS Do?		
Conjunctions hook up words, phrases, and clauses, and define the relationship between and among them.		
Connector and Function	**Example**	**Models from *Bomb* by Steve Sheinkin (2012; bold added)**
Subordinating conjunctions show relationships of condition, concession, comparison, results, or time, and usually make one idea more important than another.	*as* *although* *after* *while* *when* *until* *because* *before* *if* *since*	Oppenheimer shouldn't be allowed anywhere near the most dangerous secret in the world, argued the FBI, **because** he might leak the information to his Communist friends, and from there, to the Soviet Union. **While** other boys played in the street, Robert sat alone in his room studying languages, devouring books of literature and science, and filling notebooks with poetry.
Coordinating conjunctions organize ideas to show their equality; items joined by coordinating conjunctions are weighted equally. They join compound sentences and link pairs: *I don't like **gum or candy**.*	*for* *and* *nor* *but* *or* *yet* *so*	He was constantly getting sick, **so** his nervous parents tried to protect him by keeping him inside. The government was spending hundreds of millions of dollars—-**yet** the project was so secret, President Roosevelt chose not to tell Congress where all the money was going.

Figure 2.3
How Conjunctions Function

thought. Most of us don't know them by name, but that's not required to use relative pronouns. They are the header—or first words—of what grammarians call relative clauses. Notice that *relative* has the same root as *relationships*. Here is an example of how Sheinkin uses relative pronouns to show relationships between his ideas:

> *The map could easily be explained—he'd just say he loved Western stories, **which** was true, and **that**, out of curiosity, he'd sent to a Santa Fe museum for the map.*

The word *which*, which should always be proceeded by a comma in this usage, is unlike the word *that*, which does not require the comma. Here, *which* heads the clause that clarifies how his lie could actually be true. The word *that* connects his possession of the map to the excuse for how he obtained it. Other relative pronouns also create relationships between people and ideas (*who, whoever, whose, whom*); more examples follow in Figure 2.4.

What Do RELATIVE PRONOUNS Do?		
Relative Pronouns introduce additional information about the nouns before them.		
Function	**Example**	**Models from *Bugged* by Sarah Albee (2014; bold added)**
Links ideas and things to more detail	*that* *what* *which*	. . . [W]e'll talk about bugs **that** have been good for us, like silkworms and honeybees, and bugs **that** have been very bad for us, like the ones that spread infectious diseases.
Links people to more detail	*who* *whoever* *whose* *whom*	No matter how traumatizing it may be for the person **who** gets bitten or stung or pinched, or **who** finds half a worm waving hello from his apple, these types of bugs don't usually spread infectious diseases.

Figure 2.4
What Do Relative Pronouns Do?

Punctuation as Connectors

Punctuation choreographs and orchestrates thought.
—Jennifer DeVere Brody, *Punctuation: Art, Politics, and Play*

Connector punctuation combines, introduces, and encloses—and in so doing, often ellipts unneeded words. As all connectors do, punctuation creates cohesive relationships between ideas and signals how we should relate ideas to one another.

See how Neal Thompson (2013) uses connectors galore in this excerpt from *A Curious Man*, his biography of the creator of Ripley's Believe It or Not:

> *H. L. Mencken once said about liars: "The men that American people admire most extravagantly are the most daring liars; the men they detest the most violently are those who try to tell them the truth."*

Thompson uses a colon to *introduce* the readers to H. L. Mencken's quote. Then a semicolon is used to *combine* his two ideas. The quotation marks *enclose* the quote from Mencken, clarifying that these are his exact words. The three basic connective functions of punctuation are shown in the What Does Connector Punctuation Do? chart (see Figure 2.5).

"There are a lot of ways for writers to show relationships among ideas," I say. Handing out copies of the opening page of Steve Sheinkin's book about the Civil War, *Two Miserable Presidents: The Amazing, Terrible, and Totally True Story of the Civil War* (2009), I say, "Let's work in groups and read this passage by Steve Sheinkin. As you read, highlight how he connects ideas or shows relationships among them."

Figure 2.5
Connector punctuation has three basic functions: to combine, to introduce, and to enclose. Remember, when you enclose, you often need opening and closing marks.

What Does CONNECTOR PUNCTUATION Do?		
Combines	**Introduces**	**Encloses**
Comma **,**		Comma **,**
Dash ——	Dash ——	Dash ——
	Colon **:**	
Semicolon **;**		
		Parentheses **( )**
		Quotation Marks **" "**

On May 22, 1856, a congressman from South Carolina walked into the Senate chamber, looking for trouble. With a cane in his hand, Preston Brooks scanned the nearly empty room and spotted the man he wanted: Senator Charles Sumner of Massachusetts. Sumner was sitting at a desk, writing letters, unaware he had a visitor. He became aware a moment later, when he looked up from his papers just in time to see Preston Brooks's metal-tipped cane rising above his head.

After we read the passage, I offer, "Let's talk about the first sentence together." We reread the first sentence. "First, let's list all the ideas we see in this sentence."

On May 22, 1856, a congressman from South Carolina walked into the Senate chamber, looking for trouble.

Students note the ideas: the date, a person, where he's from, what he did, and why.

"How does Sheinkin show the relations among these ideas?" I ask.

Blank stares.

"What word introduces the date?" I ask.

"*On?*" says Aidan.

"Yes, that's a preposition," I say. "Prepositions show relationships to time, space, and examples. Are there any other places where Sheinkin uses a preposition to connect ideas?"

Students notice there is a *place* connected to a *person* with *from* (*congressman from South Carolina*), quickly noticing another preposition of *place* (*into the Senate chamber*).

"That's why you can see the word *position* in *preposition*," I say.

"What about the commas?" Desirée says, squinting. "Don't those show something?"

"Indeed they do," I say. "These commas connect. What do the commas connect?"

Blank stares.

"Look at the list of what the sentence is about," I prompt.

"Like the *why* to the *what* he did?" Sean asks.

"Yep," I say. "The comma is different from a period, which separates and ends. A comma groups and connects."

"This is hard," Mirella complains.

"Would you like a chart that will help you figure all this stuff out?"

"Yes," sneers Mercedes.

I give a copy of the complete Sheinkin paragraph and a Charting Connections handout to the groups. (See Figure 2.6 or Appendix F.) They use Charting Connections like no list that has come before.

Figure 2.6
The Charting Connections
Handout

Prepositions

What do they do? *Show time and place as well as introduce examples, contrasts, or comparisons.*

Function	Example
Time	*at, in, on*
Extended Time	*since, for, by, from, to, until, during, with(in)*
Direction	*to, toward, on, onto, in, into*
Location	*above, across, against, ahead of, along, among, around, at, by, behind, below, beside, beneath, between, from, in, inside, on, off, out of, over, near, through, toward, under, within*
Introduce Examples and Comparisons or Contrasts	*as, despite, except, for, like, of, per, than, with, without*

Relative Pronouns

What do they do? *Introduce and link additional information to the noun before it.*

Function	Example
Link **ideas and things** to more detail	*that, what, which*
Link **people** to more detail	*who, whoever, whose, whom*

Connector Punctuation

What do they do? *Combine, introduce, and enclose information.*

Combines	Introduces	Encloses
Comma **,**		Comma **,**
Dash **——**	Dash **——**	Dash **——**
Semicolon **;**	Colon **:**	Parentheses **( )**
		Quotation Marks **" "**

Subordinating Conjunctions (AAWWUBBIS)

Although
After
While
When
Until
Because
Before
If
Since

What do they do? *Show relationships, sometimes making one idea more or less important.*

Function	Example
Time	*after, before, during, since, until, when, whenever, while*
Cause-Effect	*as, because, since, so*
Opposition	*although, even though, though, while, whatever*
Condition	*as long as, if, in order to, unless, until, whatever*

Coordinating Conjunctions (FANBOYS)

For
And
Nor
But
Or
Yet
So

What do they do? *Make connections that are equal to each other. They join sentences (compound) and they can also show a relationship between a pair or a list.*

Function	Example
Combine	*and*
Opposition	*but, yet, nor*
Cause-Effect	*so, for*
Choice	*or*

In groups of three, students reread Sheinkin's paragraph and highlight the ideas in one color and the connectors in another. After about ten minutes, we talk through the passage sentence by sentence, describing the connections we see, and adding names and functions as appropriate.

It may be worth extending the lesson to help students apply this idea. If you choose to do so, we found giving them some sentences like the ones in the excerpt that follows and using the Charting Connections handout to build connections is a crucial step. If you don't extend it at this point, know that this is not a one-time lesson.

Later, to create a context, I read aloud from the beginning of another Sheinkin book, *Which Way to the Wild West? Everything Your Schoolbooks Didn't Tell You About Westward Expansion* (2010):

> *Have you ever tried to negotiate a treaty for your country? Maybe not. Well, if you ever do, play it cool. You know—don't act too eager to make a deal.*
>
> > *This would have been good advice for Robert Livingston, the American ambassador to France.*

I stop reading the passage aloud after the first five sentences of the book. To model adding connector words among and between ideas, I display the sentence that follows what I read aloud from the book, except I have decombined it from one sentence to four:

> It was afternoon.
> The date was April 11, 1803.
> Livingston was sitting in an office.
> The French foreign minister had the office.

I model thinking aloud as I revise, adding connector words to combine the ideas. "We have to think about what the relationship is between the first two ideas. I could combine the two sentences by rearranging a bit and adding a preposition. Those show time."

> **On** the afternoon **of** April 11, 1803 . . .

"Hey, look at all the words I could delete by rearranging and adding prepositions or connector words. Plus we need to use connecting punctuation after the introductory phrase. We use a comma to set off the introduction from the base clause or main idea.

"Now let's think about what was happening on the date." I think aloud. "Livingston does something. What?"

As I read through the last two sentences, I explain how *he was sitting in an office*, and then we see how we can rearrange the fourth sentence to describe the kind of office. We can use the preposition *of* to relate the office where Livingston sat to the occupant of that office.

> *On the afternoon of April 11, 1803, Livingston was sitting in the office of the French foreign minister.*

Now, in groups, students revise the following sentences, using connectors:

> The two men were chatting politely.
> Suddenly, the Frenchman cut in.
> He made an offer.
> The offer nearly knocked Livingston off his chair.

Students use the Charting Connections handout (Figure 2.6 and Appendix F) to add connectors. Groups compare their versions first, and then we look at Sheinkin's final sentence.

> *The two men were chatting politely, until the Frenchman cut in with an offer that nearly knocked Livingston out of his chair.*

We discuss how *off* and *out of* are both prepositions. In their versions, some students liked *off* better than *out of*. In addition, we discuss how the word *that* connects ideas too. I explain that they don't have to use the term *relative pronouns*, but that they do have to use relative pronouns like the words *that* or *which* or *who* to connect ideas when they talk or write or revise.

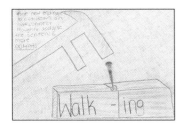

Day Four: Form New Verb Endings

The first key to exploiting verbs is to recast sentences.

—Constance Hale

Verbs move writing along, and sometimes a different form of a verb can create an opportunity for revision. Writers use participial phrases all the time. In *A Curious Man* (2013), Neal Thompson does too. He could've written two sentences about Ripley playing tennis:

Sometimes the two teamed up for doubles matches.
They won so often, they began entering citywide tournaments.

But instead he wrote one, changing the verb ending (or the irregular verb) to its participial form. Look how it helps the ideas cohere, or connect (bold added):

*Sometimes the two teamed up for doubles matches, **winning** so often they began entering citywide tournaments.*

Not a huge difference, but the two related ideas are connected rather than separated. Changing the form of the verb from *won* to *winning*, we slice off an additional *they*, get rid of a comma, and revise the sentence to its flowy goodness. We find quite often, as we go back to trim our ideas to their essential core, that this trick of shifting verb endings gives us a path to change and concision.

How do we open the door of this option to our students? We orchestrate an experience.

"I've been noticing there are lots of ways to say or write the same thing," I say. "Writers need options." I scan the classroom. "Let's figure out what some of the options are. I'll give you a hint: verbs. Watch me rework these sentences about Ripley's experience with sports."

Over the next few years Ripley would play in dozens of tournaments.
These tournaments included the annual national championship
        tournament.
They also traveled regularly to Milwaukee, Chicago, Detroit, and Cleveland.

"Everything you learn about the DRAFT mnemonic will help you revise sentences," I say, pointing toward the chart paper where we track our DRAFT mnemonic and record our learning. "Though we are focusing on the power of *forming new verb endings*, we'll call on the power of deletion, and in a way, as we change the verb endings, we are adding new connectors."

"Let's underline the verbs," I say.

Over the next few years Ripley would <u>play</u> in dozens of tournaments.
These tournaments <u>included</u> the annual national championship
        tournament.
They also <u>traveled</u> regularly to Milwaukee, Chicago, Detroit, and Cleveland.

"I'm going to leave the first verb alone because it's the main sentence. I see that the second and third verb both end in -*ed*." I stand back and look again. "Now, if I change the verb ending to the -*ing* form, I can add the ideas to the first sentence and delete some words in the process." I mark through the words I want to delete and form the new verb endings.

> ~~These tournaments~~ <u>including</u> the annual national championship tournament.
> ~~They also~~ <u>traveling</u> regularly to Milwaukee, Chicago, Detroit, and Cleveland.

"So now, I will use my main sentence first as it is and add the two participial phrases, setting them off with commas."

"And you used an *and* in a list of ideas and commas," Patricia blurts out.

"And *of*," Esmerelda says.

Here's what we ended up with, which is exactly what Thompson did. Coincidence? What do you think? Sometimes students will revise and end up matching the published text. That's not the point, but students can learn from the decisions that other writers make.

> Over the next few years Ripley would play in dozens of tournaments, including the annual national championship tournament, traveling regularly to Milwaukee, Chicago, Detroit, and Cleveland.

"Now you get a chance to revise sentences, by forming new verb endings," I say. I display the following pair of decombined sentences from Neil Gaiman's *Fortunately, the Milk*:

> Bats flew across the sky in huge flocks.
> They crowded out the waning moon.

"Remember, we're going to leave the first sentence as it is. We'll revise by merging the second sentence into the first, making one sentence. What's the first thing we do? We . . ." I wait.

"Underline the verb in the second sentence," Joseph says.

> Bats flew across the sky in huge flocks.
> They <u>crowded</u> out the waning moon.

"And now we form a new verb ending for the verb in the second sentence," I say, "changing the *-ed* to *-ing*." They compare their construction to see how it matches Gaiman's, and it does:

> *Bats flew across the sky in huge flocks, crowding out the waning moon.*

The next week my students came down with a fever—a fever for finding *-ing* verbs tumbling off the ends of sentences in their reading. A few almost squealed when they connected grammar to the real writing they read.

D R A F T

Day Five: Talk It Out

Nonfiction writers . . . often speak of the important role the ear plays in the writing and revision process. When our writing is going well, we don't worry about sentences. Guided by natural rhythms, one sentence appears, then another and another, and before we know it, we've reached the end of a paragraph. If we're lucky, the sentences will hold, the paragraph will retain its beauty and poise, and the essay will snap into place.

Then there are those other times.

——Rebecca McClanahan, "The Music of Sentences"
in Now Write! Nonfiction

When those other times occur, we don't want kids to fret over sentences, but we do want them to think them over, to consider their betterment, to make sentences that aren't working work. In short, by talking out sentences, students will make sense of their words and please their readers' ears.

One thing we've been doing all along is talking through sentences. The first part of talking it out is simply testing how sentences sound out loud, ringing true or wrecking the train. The second part is evaluative talk: the talk that analyzes, compares, and thinks through the effects of choices made and not made. So really, this is a place where all the other letters of the mnemonic come to perch, where the whole writing process, from early attempts at making sense of the words to the latter evaluation of what works and what doesn't, culminates. Though we've been doing it all along, we highlight and model this constructive collaboration and conversation in this lesson.

"Let's look back at this week," I say. "When you were given a list of simple sentences, how did you talk out what to do?"

"Huh?" José asks.

"Instead of paying attention to *deleting, rearranging, adding connectors,* and *forming new verb endings,* think about the *talk* that helped us achieve those goals."

I display an example cluster of sentences to model my thinking for students. "As I work this revision through, note the kind of talk I use."

Figure 2.7 is a T-chart. In the left-hand column, the text of the sentences is in italics. In the right-hand column, my actions are in parentheses and what I say aloud is in quotation marks. Figure 2.8 is the chart we end up with at the end of the lesson.

What Do I Say? Talk-It-Out Demonstration	
Sentences and Written Revisions	**Things I Say (and Do)**
It is biodiversity. *Biodiversity is the presence of species.* *The species are a wide variety.*	"First, I read all the sentences aloud." (I read the cluster of sentences aloud.)
	"What did you notice as I read them aloud?" (I allow response.) "So, we read it aloud to hear the repetition, the big ideas, and the potential connections or things that could go together differently." (I write *read and notice* on the Talk-It-Out chart. [See Figure 2.8.] I add and bullet *big ideas, repetitions,* and *possible connections* beneath it.)
There is a key. ~~*It is a key*~~ *to success.* ~~*The key is*~~ *for all life on earth.* *There is a key to success for all life on earth.*	"Okay, I notice the word *key* is here in all three of the first sentences. How can we put this idea together? I can delete some words because I don't need to say *key* more than once. I could say, *There is a key to success for all life on earth.* Does that make sense?" (Allow for discussion.) "Since it works, I am going to write it down. (I write out the sentence we talked out.) (After writing the sentence, I stand by the Talk-It-Out chart.) "What did we just do? We revised by . . . " (Students help name what just happened: we used strategies from DRAFT and read aloud the new sentence to see if it made sense.) "Let's add this to the chart." (I write *Revise,* bulleting *use DRAFT strategies, say possibilities aloud, write out best revisions,* and *rinse and repeat*.) (Figure 2.8)
	"Now I can see that *the key to all success for life is biodiversity,* so let's talk out how to say the rest. You could say, *There is a key to success for all life on Earth, and it is biodiversity* or we could say, *There is a key to success: biodiversity.* Or maybe I could rearrange and move *biodiversity* to the front of the sentence and say, *Biodiversity is a key to success for all life on earth.* Ooh. I like that." (I write it down.) "It makes sense."
Biodiversity is a key to success for all life on earth. ~~*Biodiversity*~~ *is the presence of species.* ~~*Species are*~~ *a wide variety.*	"Then I look at the last two sentences and look for repeated ideas and connections. One of the things I notice is that the sentence *Biodiversity is the presence of species* explains a word I already have, so I can delete *biodiversity.* The last sentence—*Species are a wide variety*—connects with the word *species,* which I already have. I can **delete** the repetitions and **rearrange**. So, talking it out: *Biodiversity, a key to success for all life on earth, is the presence of a wide variety of species.* It makes sense and I like this, so I'm going to write it." *(continued)*

Figure 2.7 In this chart, the text of the sentences is in italics in the left-hand column (except for Kurlansky's original sentence). In the right-hand column, my actions are in parentheses, and the text in quotation marks is what I said aloud.

What Do I Say? Talk-It-Out Demonstration *(continued)*	
Biodiversity, a key to success for all life on earth, is the presence of a wide variety of species.	"Now I am happy with this, but I have to see if there is another way I can say it. It's in this pushing that I start to open my mind as a writer, opening to more possibility."
	"I can rearrange *the key to success* so that it starts the sentence. Then I'd say, *A key to success for all life on earth is biodiversity, the presence of a wide variety of species.* Or I could say it this way: *Biodiversity, the presence of a wide variety of species, is a key to success for all life on earth.* Or I realize that I have two key points and can move them all over the place! I could say, *A key to success for all life on earth is biodiversity: the presence of a wide variety of species.* In this case, I use a different connector and can start thinking about the effects of my choices."
• *Biodiversity, a key to success for all life on earth, is the presence of a wide variety of species.* • *A key to success for all life on earth is biodiversity, the presence of a wide variety of species.* • *Biodiversity, the presence of a wide variety of species, is a key to success for all life on earth.* * *A key to success for all life on earth is biodiversity: the presence of a wide variety of species.*	"I write all my best revisions down and say them aloud so that I can hear how they sound. I then go back and put a star next to the one I like the best." (I write on the chart [Figure 2.8]: *Evaluate revisions*, bulleting *reread, check meaning, star best revision*, and *discuss reasons for choice*.) "You don't have to come up with four, but you do need to try with at least two. Now I have to think about which one I like the best." (I read them aloud again.) "I pick the last one because I like that it puts the *key to success* first, emphasizing it, and I like the colon. I think it makes the definition of *biodiversity* stand out. Do you want to see the original?" (I show it.)
The key to success for all life on earth is biodiversity, the presence of a wide variety of species. —Mark Kurlansky, *World Without Fish* (2011)	"So how is this different? What are the different effects of a comma introducing the definition versus a colon?"

Figure 2.7
(continued)

The chart is designed to identify where and when talk is modeled with sentences and revisions throughout the demonstration. We will be modeling our actions and thinking as we talk through this cluster of sentences decombined from Mark Kurlansky's *World Without Fish* (2011):

> It is biodiversity.
> Biodiversity is the presence of species.
> The species are a wide variety.

The power of talk in the language arts classroom can't be overstated. Revising sentences is one more place where we need to talk it out, ensuring our writing makes sense, ensuring it's economical and pleasing to the ear.

Figure 2.8
The chart is generated by students with your help. It remains up for students to refer to for their revision decisions. The easier it is for writers to refer to a chart, the more likely they are to use it.

Talk-It-Out Chart
Talk It Out!
1. Read and notice
• big ideas
• repetitions
• possible connections
2. Revise
• use DRAFT strategies
• say possibilities aloud
• write out best revisions
• rinse and repeat
3. Evaluate revisions
• reread
• check meaning
• star best revision
• discuss reasons for choice

DO YOU CATCH OUR DRAFT?

The strategies provided in DRAFT give students concrete things they can do to make their writing the best it can be by teaching options and flexibility through doable actions: deleting, rearranging, adding connectors, forming new verb endings, and talking it out.

If you reinforce or review the DRAFT strategies for revision decisions, assign groups one of the letters and its corresponding revision strategy. Once the strategies are assigned, groups create defining posters with their letter prominently featured. Remind students to be sure that the letter and the strategy words are the stars of the poster. All posters should be the same size with a consistent page layout (portrait or landscape), so that they can be hung together to spell out *DRAFT*. In this way, you can refer to this strategies mnemonic frequently as you continue your students' exploration of revision decisions.

CHAPTER

3

THE PROCESS

The Anatomy of a Revision-Decision Lesson

Great writing happens not through some dark art, but when method meets craft. The secret—if there is one—is to take one manageable step at a time . . . And then another.

  And then another.

—Jack Hart

In this chapter we offer an in-depth look at the nuts and bolts of the possibilities surrounding revision decisions as the grammar, style, and clarity unfold. Refer to this chapter both before and after you attempt the lesson sets that follow. Each lesson's structure is patterned for student success.

We break down the elements that work together in the revising process, answering the *what, how,* and *why.* First, in the Revision-Decision Lesson Structure chart (Figure 3.1), we name each element of the revision process we use in the lesson sets, explaining what it is and why it's necessary. Following the chart is an elaborated narrative with vignettes containing teacher and student talk to give a feel for each element's application and to support its implementation. (Appendixes A through E support the sample lesson described in Chapter 3. Appendixes F and G are charts referred to in various lesson sets in Part 2.)

WHAT'S THE CONTEXT?

To begin, we set a context by giving writers a reason or need for the structures they may encounter in revising and combining sentences in the lesson.

Revision-Decision Lesson Structure		
Section	**What Is It?**	**Why?**
The Context	• Provides a reason or need for skill. • Offers a writing issue that needs to be solved. • Demonstrates *where* and *how* the skill fits within the process of making meaning.	Students engage when they can easily see the need for a skill and understand how it fits into the larger picture of writing and communication.
The Points of Emphasis	• Names and highlights grammar structures likely to be encountered while revising sentences. • Eases cross-referencing with school, district, state, or national standards or expectations.	Information about curricular grammar goals possible in the lesson helps teachers know which concepts they can, if needed, emphasize or brush up on before the lesson.
The Demonstration	• Models the revising of sentences and more. • Models the possible decisions writers make and how they generate them. • Reveals concrete ways to improve writing and solve a writer's problems. • Models *talk-it-out* process.	Students need to see the target to reach it successfully. The same is true for writing behaviors. If they haven't seen writing behaviors patterned before their eyes, they can't always pull them out of the sky. Modeling shows rather than tells.
The Practice	• Provides a structured opportunity for writers to get their feet wet, playing and experimenting with the work of revision. • Engages students at a deeper level, since revising through grammar is one solution.	Since everyone works on the same sentence, this practice gives more opportunities for shared discussion and—once again—demonstrates that there are many possible outcomes or decisions.
The Collaboration	• Seeks a group solution to construct clear and concise sentences and paragraphs. • Engages students in collaborative meaning making. • Encourages talk and reflective learning.	Cooperative groups create new conversations and learning. Creating writing together and comparing and contrasting versions causes generative and analytic talk. Reflection cements and clarifies concepts.
The Application	• Provides concrete ways to nudge students into using the skills discussed and discovered to solve their own writing problems. • Sends students back to their own writing to apply the skill.	Revision becomes an integrated part of the writing program when students are nudged to practically apply it to their own composition process.

Figure 3.1 This chapter elaborates on this model used in the ten lesson sets that follow.

Often the power of comparison and contrast is used, making the need for a skill clear to students. Research-based instruction (Marzano, Pickering, and Pollock 2007) reminds us that comparison-contrast is the most effective teaching strategy across all curriculum areas. We can also use other strategies to highlight tools and structures of language to raise students' awareness of why we bother with learning about grammar and style. Most often, we take a target sentence and then rewrite it or find a contrasting example as a way to establish the context for students or to introduce them to a grammar concept through revision.

The context section focuses on one or two of the points of emphasis—not all of them. We never want to give students a sip of water from a fire hose (Anderson 2005).

For instance, you know you have to deal with participles because your curriculum says so—but more than that, writers need to know participles are a nifty tool we use. Participles and participial phrases solve problems for us as writers almost every day, ***helping*** *us combine sentences,* ***adding*** *clarity and variety,* ***keeping*** *our writing moving.* Useful. So how do we create a need for participles? That's the purpose of the context section, seeing where the skill fits into the process of writing or meaning making as a whole. A need plus the proper place or setting for the skill is initiated.

Here is an example of what you'll find in the lesson sets.

The Context

"I've been reading this book about a horrible, history-making fire in a clothing or garment factory back in 1911," I say. "The book builds to the climax when the factory catches fire, leaving many employees trapped. As I've read, I've noticed a couple of things Albert Marrin does to keep the action moving."

I step forward, book in hand. "It's called *Flesh and Blood So Cheap: The Triangle Fire and Its Legacy* [2011]. When the book is getting tense as the fire starts, you want to see what's happening. You want action. How can you put more action in a sentence? Let's look at these two versions. What do you notice?"

Flames shot up, igniting the line of hanging paper patterns.

Flames shot up into the air.
The flames ignited paper patterns that were hanging.
The patterns were on a line that hung across the room.

"I think the second one is better because it gives you more information," Jon says.
"What is the added information?" I ask.

The class pauses, then squints, then some tilt their heads to the side. I wait this out.

"Well, when I start looking for something new, I don't really see that much," Jon says. "It's just more words."

"I know," I say. "Sometimes we think more is better. It can be, but it certainly isn't always. The point is we want whatever words we end up using to do some work. And, if we can say the same thing in fewer words, that's often better, especially in informational writing."

I move toward the screen where the sentences are projected. "Let's focus on parts of the sentences."

"*Flames shot up*," I say, pointing to the first sentence, "versus *Flames shot up into the air*." I move my hand to the second sentence. "Why is one better than the other? Let's take a vote. Which one is better, the first or second? Raise one finger for the first one and two fingers for the second version."

Most students vote for the first.

"Okay. Why do you think most of us voted for the first version?" I look around the room.

"Well, *flames shot up* really already tells you they went up in the air. I mean, where else would they go? You don't need *in the air*. That's dumb," Anya says.

"So, if I am trying to be concise, or to the point, or keep the action moving, less is better?"

"Sure," Nicole says, shrugging.

Here is one of those times I need to remember the adage "The one who is talking is doing the work." The most important part of these activities is letting the students discover as much as they can. It's like being schooled in wait time—ten seconds minimum, oftentimes more. Revision decisions are a great training ground, because after ten, even twenty seconds, well-thought-out answers flow, if only at a trickle sometimes. Remember the Grand Canyon started with a trickle. Trickles deepen. Eventually.

We continue our discussion.

I do jump in with some direct instruction, explaining how Albert Marrin uses *igniting* versus *ignited* and how he can change the structure of his sentence and add multiple actions to it without making a list. Participles love to tumble off the ends of sentences (see Tip Box).

*Flames shot up, **igniting** the line of hanging paper patterns.*

Francis Christensen (2007) said sentences with participial phrases tumbling off the end are one of the most used patterns in modern writing and one of the easiest for novice writers to navigate.

The context sections of the lesson sets that follow show one approach to beginning the lesson. Depending on the focus the teacher chooses, the context may change from one class to another. The point is to prepare students for the learning that will follow by providing background or examples or situations, so that students see a reason for the learning and how this skill fits into the big picture of making meaning.

Throughout the lessons, tip boxes like this offer background information to enhance talk about issues that might emerge in revision-decision discussions.

 Tip | **Verbal or *-ing* Verb?**

Technically a participle is a verbal, not a verb, but we, under the guidance of our mentor, Harry Noden, have found much success by referring to it as an *-ing* verb (present participles). Yes, the participle can also end in *-en* or *-ed* (past participles), but as Noden describes in *Image Grammar* (2011), it is best to wait and let students discover that fact naturally, rather than overload them with a grammar-information dump that makes grammar skills seem unattainable.

DISCOVERING SENTENCES TO REVISE

How do teachers select text passages? We continually keep our eyes (and ears) open for passages with sentences that are interesting and that model a useful syntactical structure. (See Figure 3.2. Words and phrases in bold indicate targeted structures.)

Figure 3.2

Interesting Sentences That Model Targeted Structures	
Appositives	The electric caterpillar, **a type of stinging caterpillar**, is the larva of a moth that lives in southern Brazil. —Steve Jenkins, *Never Smile at a Monkey* (2009a) The jail smelled of concrete—**a cold, damp scent like the inside of a cave**. —Silas House, *The Coal Tattoo* (2005)
Commas in a series	It's composed of **dead plankton, fish scales, animal waste, and bits of larger creatures** that have died in the waters above. —Steve Jenkins, *Down, Down, Down* (2009b) His hands smelled of **suitcase, metal, *Mein Kampf*, and survival**. ——Markus Zusak, *The Book Thief* (2007)
Participial Phrases	He turned over, **tugging at his sheet**. ——Sheila Turnage, *Three Times Lucky* (2012) Flames shot up, **igniting the line of hanging paper patterns**. –Albert Marrin, *Flesh and Blood So Cheap* (2011)

There Is No Right Way to Decombine	
Marrin's Sentence: *A rat can collapse its skeleton, allowing it to wriggle through a hole as narrow as three-quarters of an inch.*	
Debbie's Decombining	**Jeff's Decombining**
A rat can do something. It can collapse its skeleton. Doing that allows it to wriggle. It wriggles through small holes. Holes can be as narrow as three-quarters of an inch.	A rat can make itself smaller. A rat gets smaller by collapsing its skeleton. Getting smaller allows the rat to wriggle through holes. The holes can be narrow. The holes can be as narrow as three-quarters of an inch.
Jeff's combination of Debbie's sentence cluster: A rat can collapse its skeleton and wriggle through small holes as narrow as three-quarters of an inch.	**Debbie's combination of Jeff's sentence cluster:** A rat can make itself smaller by collapsing its skeleton, allowing it to get through holes as narrow as three-quarters of an inch.

Figure 3.3
Note that although we decombined the sentences in different ways, the sentences we created for revision weren't incorrect; they were just complete sentences that could be combined.

After we find passages, we transform them into sentence sets, dividing the content into a cluster of short, complete sentences. (See Figure 3.3.) The cluster of sentences we create can be revised into one sentence. We want students to spend their time with correct sentences, but we try to isolate bits of information in each one, showing how multiple ideas are embedded in each sentence.

Some teachers worry that they won't do the decombining "correctly," but there isn't a single "right way" to do this. To demonstrate, we each created a cluster of sentences from the same published sentence in *Oh, Rats! The Story of Rats and People* by Albert Marrin (2006). It's clear that we decombined the same sentence differently. And that's okay. Really.

In our revisions, neither of us matched the original sentence exactly, and that's fine, too. Exact matching is *not* the point. From this example, we can see how the way we decombine might cue students in certain directions. That's something to consider but not to worry about. If you are hoping students will learn to combine to create a specific grammatical structure (appositives, participial phrases, adjectives in a series), realize that the point is flexibility in reformulation. They don't need to all match one answer. That's not composition. That's a worksheet. In general, whatever helps students consider a variety of ways to revise ideas to make meaning is beneficial, inviting them to discover that different syntactical choices create different effects.

WHAT ARE THE POINTS OF EMPHASIS?

To anchor us in what might likely arise during a lesson, we identify many of the types of structures for the sample lesson that follows (see Figure 3.4).

Pick one or two only. As with all revision-decision endeavors, you can teach a variety of concepts. Of course, students won't identify every element listed in the points of emphasis. Some of what they identify might have to do with the context teachers establish or the students' readiness for other concepts. It's about natural meaning making, about meeting students' needs with one or more of the possibilities listed here. If everything is emphasized, then nothing is.

Teachers make decisions about which points are appropriate to focus on or emphasize and which may be left for later. You can always revisit sentences and patterns. In fact, it's necessary to do so. We don't want to drown students in abstract terms and memorization; instead, we want to help students understand these concepts as a way to make meaning as much as to navigate their use to make meaning. Multiple possibilities for discussion exist in texts.

Figure 3.4 shows how we built the points of emphasis for the sample lessons so that teachers can build their own lessons beyond those in this book. First, find an interesting passage in a text students are reading, will read, or might want to read. Then identify possibilities of language they could learn from the passage, sentence by sentence.

Figure 3.4
This merely shows the possibility of what could be discussed when studying these sentences from Albert Marrin's *Flesh and Blood So Cheap* (2011). We shouldn't crowd our discussion with too much abstract lingo or terms or points. Select a point and *emphasize*, one or two things at the most.

Elaborated Points of Emphasis with Links to Text
First, the invention of the sprinkler made it possible to drown a fire in seconds. • Introductory word set off with a comma (*First,*) • Independent clause (*The invention of the sprinkler made it possible to drown a fire in seconds.*) • Prepositional phrases (**of** *the sprinkler,* **in** *seconds*) • Infinitive phrases (**to drown** *a fire*)
Sprinklers, attached to ceilings, had sensitive fuses. • Independent clause (*Sprinklers had sensitive fuses.*) • Past participial phrase (**attached** *to ceilings*)
Heat rising from a fire triggered the fuses, which automatically released a deluge of water stored in overhead sprinkler pipes. • Independent clause (*Heat triggered the fuses.*) • Participial phrases (Present participle: **rising** *from a fire.* Past participle: **stored** *in overhead sprinkler pipes*) • Relative clause (**which** *automatically released a deluge of water*) • Prepositional phrases (**from** *a fire;* **in** *overhead sprinkler pipes*)

The Points of Emphasis

In the ten lesson sets that follow Chapter 3, rather than parroting all the goals each time, we cut them to the quick so you can easily identify what's possible. The material in Figure 3.4 is condensed to this:

- Participle
- Infinitive
- Prepositional phrase
- Subordinate clause

Teachers can use the same process we modeled in Figure 3.4, choosing from all the possibilities those that would be most appropriate for their students and that should receive the most emphasis.

WHAT'S THE DEMONSTRATION?

The demonstration gives teachers a chance to model thinking and decision making at the point of revision. Recasting sentences, using replicable strategies students can also use, is the goal of the demonstration. As Cris Tovani (2000) says, we make the invisible visible.

The Demonstration

"Do you remember our revision-decision mnemonic for some options writers have when combining sentences?" I ask.

"DRAFT," several students say.

We review what strategy each letter represents:

Delete unnecessary and repeated words.
Rearrange sentence parts/chunks.
Add connectors.
Form new verb endings.
Talk it out.

We consistently remind students that we use the word *DRAFT* because it connotes the impermanence of what we are doing. We are drafting—deleting when we need to, rearranging for effect, adding connector words to cohere, forming new verb endings when we delete repetition or change positions, and, most important, using the wide resources of syntax we have in our own speech. We talk it out again and again, reformulating and redrafting until we arrive at our intended meaning. We are in the act of creation, in the process of discovery—not looking for one right or correct answer.

"What are some possibilities for combining this first set?" I ask.

> The invention of the sprinkler created possibilities.
> It was possible to drown a fire.
> It would take only seconds.

Students talk out a few answers, we listen, and we think about what makes sense. We discuss the troublesome overused *it*. One group wonders if we should move the prepositional phrase *in seconds* to the front of the sentence. We celebrate this attempt. Phrases and clauses can be rearranged, and we want writers to see possibilities and to analyze what works better.

> In only seconds, the invention of the sprinkler created possibilities to drown a fire.

"Let's reread this and think about what it means," I say. "This is always part of the process. We try sentences several ways: we talk them out and we reflect on them to make sure they say what we intend."

"Well," Shaundra says, "it kind of sounds like the invention only took seconds, and I know that isn't true, because inventions take a long time to come out right, and they usually don't get it the first time."

"Yeah, plus it's saying it takes the sprinklers seconds to put out the fire," Troy says. "The invention didn't happen in two seconds."

"Two great things just happened here," I say. "One, you realized the flexibility of rearranging phrases and clauses, and two, you see how we can change the meaning in unintended ways—sometimes—when we do that." After a discussion on placement and meaning and a few other options, the class decides on this version:

> The invention of the sprinkler created possibilities to drown a fire in only seconds.

Unless students need more modeling, let them work in small groups to revise the next cluster or pair of sentences. These are fairly simple, and it's ideal to put students in the driver's seat.

> Sprinklers were attached to ceilings.
> Sprinklers had sensitive fuses.

I overhear some students noting that both sentences start with *sprinklers*. One student argues that writers often repeat words for emphasis. Eventually, they decide that emphasis is not really appropriate here, so they delete one *sprinklers*.

In this kind of sentence play, it's easy to misplace modifiers. One group writes, *Sprinklers were attached to ceilings, which had sensitive fuses.*

"Let's talk about this revision," I say. "It's a really strong effort to use the *which* clause. I think we could just leave it, but something in me says to reread it and make sure it says what we mean. Does anybody see where someone might be confused by this version?"

When they all say no, I point out that in actuality, modifiers are all about location, what they are near. When we put the phrase *which had sensitive fuses* next to *ceilings*, it can sound like the ceilings have the fuses, because that's what's closest to the phrase.

Now they see it. I don't do this to correct the students. It is another opportunity to see that while drafting sentences, we constantly check and recheck meaning to ensure it isn't lost or changed in translation. Revision is a problem-solving process.

We continue this discussion. "Now that we know we can move phrases and clauses, is there another place we can move *attached to ceilings* and still have it make sense?" I ask.

"If it needs to be by the word it's describing," Ryan comments, "then it can really only be before or after *sprinklers*, right?"

"Good point. So . . . ?" I wait.

"You could say *attached to ceilings, sprinklers had sensitive fuses,*" says Joseph.

"Way to talk it out, Joseph. Anything else?" After my painful thirty seconds of wait time, I share one other possibility that they aren't seeing yet: *Sprinklers, attached to ceilings, had sensitive fuses.* I write it on the board so they can see the comma rule in action. I will come back tomorrow and name this and put it on our chart of sentence options.

"We can say, *Attached to ceilings, sprinklers had sensitive fuses* or *Sprinklers, attached to ceilings, had sensitive fuses.* What is the difference?"

"They both make sense," Patrice says, "but I think the one where *sprinklers* starts the sentence and stands by itself makes it look more important."

"It gives it more emphasis," I say.

We finally agree on this version: *Sprinklers, attached to ceilings, had sensitive fuses.*

WHAT'S THE PRACTICE?

The practice provides students with a hands-on, minds-on opportunity to attempt skills with peers, exploring what works and sometimes what doesn't. Learning happens at the point of use, and this practice is ripe for teachable moments. The act of reformulating, with all its false starts and aha moments, tells students two things: what problems need to be solved and what strategies they can use. Fluent revising comes with doing the work of revising. It's messy. It's active processing. Mistakes will be made. But the concrete actions demonstrated now become a part of students' repertoires as writers to lean on again and again as they make decisions, refining and polishing their words to a high sheen.

Emphasis on Meaning, Not Correctness

Discussion about sentence elements in these lessons relates more to meaning than correctness. In each grammatical example, we analyze why the author chose to include the information in a phrase or clause instead of in a separate sentence, and how its placement would contribute to meaning in the particular sentence. This flexible discussion of choice and possibility is essential.

As we discuss phrases and clauses the students study, we discover that they serve a variety of purposes: to add information is most common, but they can also be used to create rhythm and clarity. Here are some questions we can use in these discussions:

- Why don't we just combine the two sentences with *and* or another coordinating conjunction?
- Why do we take out repeated words?
- Why do we take out words, phrases, or clauses?
- Why do we rearrange them or put them in different spots?
- Why do we change the endings of verbs when we put them in new spots or delete words?
- How does this (arrangement, choice, placement, etc.) change the meaning?
- Why would we, as authors, at times choose not to make any of these revisions?

The Practice

Not all sentence-revision sets are created equal. After the experience with the last sentence and because of the next sentence's complexity, I adjust, and lead students through another revision of the next set of sentences as a group.

"What are some ways we could revise the following cluster of sentences?" I ask. "What are some things to think about as we do so?"

Heat rose from the fire.
The heat triggered the fuses.
The fuses automatically released a deluge of water.
The water had been stored in overhead sprinkler pipes.

"I think they sound just fine the way they are," Aidan says, yawning.

"Some authors might. Because they are all correct sentences, aren't they?" I say. "But let's listen to them when we read them aloud. What do you hear?"

Students notice that the flow is singsong-y, choppy, repetitious. Actually, I share those words to help them as they search for ways to name what's "off."

"What's something we can delete from the first two sentences?"

"Take out *heat*," Santiago says.

"Okay. Somebody talk that out for me." I want to nudge students to talk out sentences in class because that is my expectation of them when they work in small groups. If I don't model that now, while I am there to support them, they won't do it when they work in groups or independently.

"*Heat rose from the fire and triggered the fuses*," Ariel says.

"Is there another way we can revise? What about *form new verb endings*?" I point to the DRAFT poster. "Are there any verbs we can change the form of?"

When no one else mentions it, I suggest, *Heat rising from the fire triggered the fuses*, but students like the first combination. "We've got a start; let's look at the other sentences. How can we add them or combine them?"

"Well, it repeats *fuses*," Ralph offers.

"Then we can probably delete that, right?

"Write this on the board," Janie says. "*Heat rose from the fire, triggering the fuses to release a deluge of water*."

"You are making this sentence really interesting. What about the last sentence? What should we do with that?"

"It's repeating again. Repeating means deleting," Aidan says.

"You're a poet and didn't know it," I say, smiling. "If we take out *water*, how do we connect this last sentence to some of the revisions we have so far?"

"I want to add it to your sentence. The one we already added to." Pearl points to *Heat rose from the fire, triggering the fuses to release a deluge of water.* "Add *that was stored in overhead pipes*."

We stand back and look at the sentence.

Heat rose from the fire, triggering the fuses to release a deluge of water that was stored in overhead pipes.

"Could we use *which* instead of *that*?" Marvin asks.

"Talk it out."

After some discussion (and a switch from *that* to *which*), we take all three sentences and look at them.

Part of our collaboration is to compare and contrast. This gets talk flowing and reflections growing. We compare our version with what Albert Marrin wrote in *Flesh and Blood So Cheap*—not for the right answer, but for a discussion of the effects of the options he chose. Comparisons help us see that other writers make revision decisions.

First, the invention of the sprinkler made it possible to drown a fire in seconds. Sprinklers, attached to ceilings, had sensitive fuses. Heat rising from a fire triggered the fuses, which automatically released a deluge of water stored in overhead sprinkler pipes.

We talk about the differences and similarities and the effects of authors' choices, and as usual, many students like their own combinations better.

WHAT'S THE COLLABORATION?

The goal of this process is not only to revise, but also to practice the skills of sentence variety and flexibility. What follows are directions along with sample sentence sets teachers can use as a model to guide their own students' collaboration and conversation around revision decisions.

The Collaboration

Groups of three or four students each get one cluster of sentences. Some groups will get the same sentence cluster. This will help emphasize that this work is about combining to make meaning rather than about a search for one right answer.

Cluster 1

It took minutes.
146 workers died.
They ended up broken on the sidewalk.
Others were suffocated by smoke.
Many were burnt in the flames.

Cluster 2

Most were young women.
They were ages fourteen to twenty-three.
Nearly all were recent immigrants.
They were mostly Italians and Russian Jews.

Cluster 3

It was dubbed the "Triangle Fire."
It held the record for New York's deadliest workplace fire.
It held the record for ninety years.

Cluster 4

Only the September 11, 2001, terrorist attacks took more lives.
Those attacks were on the World Trade Center.

Students revise their assigned cluster into one or two sentences, using the DRAFT strategies that have been previously modeled. Remember to have an anchor chart on the wall that you can point to and remind students of their options for revising. When students have finished creating at least two different revisions of their sentences, they star one and read them in the order of the numbered clusters. Each sentence may be written on chart paper or displayed using any technology.

Students share their revisions, and the class compares the sentences that were combined in different ways, noting different choices and effects. Here is Albert Marrin's original paragraph as it appears in *Flesh and Blood So Cheap*:

> *Within minutes, 146 workers died, broken on the sidewalk, suffocated by smoke, or burnt in the flames. Most were young women ages fourteen to twenty-three, nearly all recent immigrants, Italians and Russian Jews. Dubbed the "Triangle Fire," for ninety years it held the record as New York's deadliest workplace fire. Only the September 11, 2001, terrorist attacks on the World Trade Center took more lives.*

WHAT'S THE APPLICATION?

Writers often need a nudge to apply new things they learn. To help them stretch, we push them back into their reading and writing, scouring for opportunities to apply the skills discovered through sentence revision:

- Find a part of your writing you want to revise and apply something we've studied to your own writing.
- Note a particular structure in your reading. Next time you revise sentences, see if you can use it.
- Use DRAFT actions to make any piece of writing strong and clear.
- Write a reflection about using DRAFT or any skill we have addressed to make your writing better.

The Application

First, we want students to notice in their reading the structures we've studied and worked with as a class. For example, if students read the following passage from *The Hunger Games* (Collins 2010), we hope they might notice the underlined words after this lesson.

> *When I wake up, the other side of the bed is cold. My fingers stretch out, <u>seeking Prim's warmth but finding only the rough canvas cover of the mattress.</u> She must have had bad dreams and climbed in with our mother. Of course, she did. This is the day of the reaping.*

We suggest that students write some of these sentences and their effects in their notebooks. A student made this entry in her writer's notebook:

> I like the second sentence of the Hunger Games because it has three actions that aren't really in a list. The other –ing words act like adjectives, I think, describing what her fingers did. I could use –ing verbs in my own writing when I want to squeeze a lot of actions in one sentence.

We also want to remind students, as they return to their writing in progress, to use some of the structures we've noticed and talked about for the effects we've discussed. We could show them an example of what that might look like:

> *Earlier draft:* Escaping from the zombie, the girl ran to the door and banged on it hard. She hoped someone would answer quickly, and she glanced behind her as she waited to see if her followers were too close.

> *Revised draft:* The girl ran to the door and banged on it, hoping someone would answer quickly, glancing behind her to see if her followers were too close.

THE REVISION-DECISION LESSONS THAT FOLLOW

The ten lessons that follow all reflect the process described in this chapter and explore a variety of craft principles and grammatical structures. Although the lessons follow the pattern of *the context* through *the application* as elaborated on in this chapter, the lessons in Part 2 are streamlined for ease of use. Be flexible. Don't forget that your students' reactions and questions should guide the speed at which you travel and the depth to which you plunge. What we offer is a scaffold for you to use as you need it.

PART 2

The Lesson Sets

This journey helped me to understand the need to teach grammar in an artist's studio. This means allowing for studio time when students can practice their art, writing with models . . . It means discussing the art of the masters, posting their passages, and sharing insights from reading in small-group discussions and individual conferences.

—Harry Noden, *Image Grammar*

LESSON SET

MODIFYING IN THE RIGHT DIRECTION
Right-Branching Sentences

Writers grow sentences. They start with a sentence that is direct and clear like this one from *Creep and Flutter: The Secret World of Insects and Spiders* by Jim Arnosky (2012):

Honeybees create hives.

Then they grow the sentence by adding more words. But not just to make a sentence longer. What they add (shown here in bold) enhances meaning and information.

*Honeybees create hives, **labyrinths of wax honeycomb in which they store honey and raise their young**.*

In this case, Arnosky's modification comes after the main sentence or base clause. The modifiers give us a visual of what hives are made of, what they look like, and what they are used for. When modifying or describing details are added at the end of a sentence, we call this a right-branching sentence, because the information branches out to the right. In *Mechanically Inclined* (Anderson 2005), a right-branching sentence is referred to as a *closer*. That term refers to the modification's location and the way in which it finishes or closes the sentence.

As writers, we learn from Jim Arnosky to be careful not to overload our main sentence with too much information, but rather to branch out steps to the right that tell us more information, not in complete sentences but in clauses and phrases, nouns and adjectives, all of which deepen readers' understanding of the initial main sentence. In Arnosky's sentence, the new right-branching information is an appositive, but other grammatical structures, such as prepositions and participles, can do the same work in modifying the base clause. Remember the sentence we studied from *Oh, Rats! The Story of Rats and People* (2006) by Albert Marrin?

A rat can collapse its skeleton, <u>allowing</u> it to wriggle through a hole as narrow as three-quarters of an inch.

Discuss how the bold right branch or closer adds to the base sentence in this example. Notice that the Marrin example is a participial phrase (or -*ing* phrase) that tells about the rats' specific actions to modify the broader point that rats collapse their skeletons.

Consider this example, also from Arnosky:

*Bees, wasps, and ants belong to an order of insects called Hymenoptera, **which means "membranous wings."***

The familiar serial comma is in the first part of the sentence, allowing Arnosky to pack more examples in, but what's interesting is the way he uses another grammatical structure, a relative clause because it's headed with the relative pronoun *which*. The relative clause explains and renames, somewhat like an appositive, but with a *which* or *who* to kick it off. It doesn't matter so much what writers name it. What matters is that they know these "*which* or *who* additions" are another option they can use to modify and clarify a sentence with relevant detail.

What can writers learn from these examples about right-branching sentences? They can articulate understanding that different right-branching structures, in the end, do the same thing: modify the main sentence without crowding it with adjectives and adverbs.

 ## Relative Pronouns and What They Clause

Relative pronouns—such as *who, whoever, whose, whom, which,* and *that*—are used to head relative clauses. A relative clause links the noun that proceeds it to the additional information or modification. Relative clauses act as adjectives, explaining more about the noun they follow like in these right-branching examples (in bold) from Nicola Davies's *What's Eating You? Parasites—The Inside Story* (2009):

*Human tapeworms have an even more complicated method of getting into a human body, **which relies on their changing body shape three times on their journey!***

*Inside a pig or cow, they hatch into little hooked blobs, **which wiggle into the blood and ride around until they get to a muscle.***

THE POINTS OF EMPHASIS

- Participles (Verbal)
- Absolutes
- Relative pronouns and clauses
- Nonessential parenthetical elements
- Commas separating items and actions in a series

THE DEMONSTRATION

To demonstrate how to create right-branching sentences, display the following simple sentence clusters, derived from sentences in the Newbery Honor book *Three Times Lucky* by Sheila Turnage (2012):

> He turned over.
> He tugged.
> He was tugging at his sheet.

> Dale sat bolt upright.
> His blue eyes were round.
> His hair was blond.
> His hair was spiking in all directions.

We practice revising these sentences by starting with a clear sentence or base clause, and then adding modification or information to the right. The additions should tell the reader more about the main sentence or base clause.

As we read these first three sentences, we leave the first sentence as the main sentence or action.

> He turned over.

Now we look at the other two sentences. We see we can use the *F* from the DRAFT mnemonic to *form new verb endings* and use either *tugged* or *tugging*. We try to head the phrase with the participle *tugging*. Now we can delete *He tugged* and *He was*. We need a comma after the main sentence or base clause to show we're adding to it.

> He turned over, **tugging at his sheet.**

Does that capture the meaning in the three sentences? Does that make the image of him turning over clearer? *Tugging at his sheet* is a participial phrase that modifies or tells us more about the main sentence *He turned over*.

Let's try the other one. We can leave the first short sentence again as the main sentence or action, then add all the modification to the right.

> Dale sat bolt upright.

There's a great writing trick you can do if you're adding phrases that don't need to be a whole sentence. And we don't need these other three sentences to be whole sentences because we already have one (*Dale sat bolt upright*). Again, we are adding the information from these three sentences to an already complete sentence.

> His blue eyes were round.
> His hair was blond.
> His hair was spiking in all directions.

Let's take the first sentence about his eyes. If you delete the verb of being from this sentence, we can start the phrase with the pronoun *his* that refers to the sentence before it and create a new construction: the absolute.

> his blue eyes round

We can pair up the other two sentences about his hair with this one, starting the phrase in a parallel way, with the pronoun *his*.

> Dale sat bolt upright, **his** blue eyes round and **his** blond hair spiking in all directions.

Tip · Absolute Modification: A Right-Branching Option

When we deleted the verb of being, *were*, from *his blue eyes were round*, it was no longer a complete sentence. Instead, we created an **absolute**: *his blue eyes round.* We can add an absolute to the end of a sentence to modify the sentence that precedes it. In this case, the sentence ended in two absolutes because *his blond hair spiking in all directions* is also an absolute phrase. Harry Noden (2011) simplifies the definition of an absolute to a *noun + an -ing verb*, which works for the second one: *his blond **hair spiking** in all directions.* But the first absolute is a *noun + adjectives.* An absolute can be a *noun + prepositions* as well: Sentences using absolutes can be powerful, *noun phrases clarifying images at the end of a sentence.*

THE PRACTICE

Students tussle with the following simple sentence clusters with a partner, making revision decisions. They use DRAFT strategies to delete unnecessary repetition, rearrange sentence chunks, add connectors, or form new verb endings. Though they write two revisions and star the one they like best, they should always talk the sentences out to make sure they make sense.

He looked around the café.
It was deserted.
The 7UP clock ticked.
It was loud and lonely.
It was on the far wall.

Students share revisions, comparing and contrasting different responses, then finally compare their writing with Turnage's original, remembering we look only to see other options, not for a correct answer.

He looked around the deserted café as the 7UP clock ticked loud and lonely on the far wall.

Students may be surprised that Turnage didn't use any of the forms we talked about to add modification. Some may be particularly disturbed that there is no comma in the sentence. Again. Different. Options. And we celebrate the differences and relish the different effects we have the options to create in our writing.

Students evaluate similarities and differences between their own versions and the author's and the effects created by the different options. We discuss their process, considering the following questions:

- What helped you most to revise the sentences? What did you learn about revising?
- Why doesn't it matter if your sentence doesn't match the original? What differences do various constructions create?
- What are some patterns you noticed?
- Where would you use these patterns in your own writing? How would they help you as a writer?
- What questions do you still have?

Essential and Nonessential

I think Strunk and White finally got through to me on whether a clause or phrase is essential (not set off by a comma or commas if it interrupts a sentence) or nonessential, which is set off by a comma or commas. Think about this common truism: *People who live in glass houses shouldn't throw stones.* The clause *who live in glass houses* is essential to the meaning of the sentence, because if we take it out, what we're left with (*People shouldn't throw stones*) doesn't communicate the sentence's point. If, on the other hand, the clause is not necessary, it is set off with a comma or commas. Here are two examples of

nonessential phrases from April Pulley Sayre's *Here Come the Humpbacks!* (2013):

Whales, **like people**, are mammals.

Toothed whales, **such as orcas**, use their sharp teeth to catch fish and other prey.

THE COLLABORATION

Distribute the following sentence sets based on text in a book about World War II, Laura Hillenbrand's *Unbroken: A World War II Story of Survival, Resilience, and Redemption* (2010). Sentences are grouped into clusters that can be revised into one sentence. For example, all the sentences in 1.1 could make one sentence. The second number indicates the order in which the sentences will form a paragraph.

Groups revise their assigned sentence in at least two ways and then select their favorite.

1.1 It was before dawn and still dark.
    It was August 26, 1929.
    A boy was in the back of a small house.
    It was in Torrance, California.
    The boy was twelve years old.
    He sat up in bed.
    He listened.

1.2 There was a sound.
    It was coming from outside.
    The sound was growing.
    It grew ever louder.

1.3 It was huge.
    It was a rush.
    The rush was heavy.
    It suggested immensity.
    It suggested a great parting of air.

1.4 It was coming from directly above the house.
    The boy swung his legs.
    He swung them off his bed.
    He raced down the stairs.
    He slapped open the back door.
    He loped onto the grass.

1.5 The yard was otherworldly.
The yard was smothered in darkness.
The darkness was unnatural.
The yard was shivering with sound.

1.6 The boy stood on the lawn.
He was beside his brother.
His brother was older.
His head was thrown back.
He was spellbound.

Groups share their sentences, displaying them so that everyone can see them and putting them in order as a paragraph, revising for flow as needed. Compare the class's constructions to Hillenbrand's original text from *Unbroken.* What effects are created by each choice?

> *In the predawn darkness of August 26, 1929, in the back of a small house in Torrance, California, a twelve-year-old boy sat up in bed, listening. There was a sound coming from outside, growing ever louder. It was a huge, heavy rush, suggesting immensity, a great parting of air. It was coming from directly above the house. The boy swung his legs off his bed, raced down the stairs, slapped open the back door, and loped onto the grass. The yard was otherworldly, smothered in unnatural darkness, shivering with sound. The boy stood on the lawn beside his older brother, head thrown back, spellbound.*

THE APPLICATION

Go Sentence Shopping

Students collect three right-branching sentences to share with a group. Writers shop textbooks or independent reading for sentences that start with a base clause or main idea, and then have modifications or additions that branch out to the right. If the class has a blog or a Twitter account, sentences can also be posted there.

Here are examples of right-branching sentences from Jonah Lehrer's *How We Decide* (2010; bold added):

> *This division of mind is one of Plato's most enduring themes,* **an idea enshrined in Western culture.**

> *On the one hand, humans are part animal,* **primitive beasts stuffed full of primitive desires.**

> *And yet, humans are also capable of reason and foresight,* **blessed with the divine gift of rationality.**

Right-branching **participial phrases** gracefully tumble off the end of Charles C. Mann's sentences in *Before Columbus: The Americas of 1491* (2009; bold added):

> *More than 50 rivers plunge down from the Andes,* **cutting through the coastal desert on their way to the Pacific.**

> *She uncovered 150 structures,* **including big stone buildings with apartments.**

> *[Fertilizer runoff] causes an excess growth of the tiny plants known as algae,* **unbalancing the ecosystem.**

I'll Show You My Sentences . . .

Once students have collected their three right-branching sentences, they share them in small groups. Groups categorize types of sentences they collected, naming, comparing, and contrasting. The class discusses and clarifies discoveries, attempting to use grammatical terms if helpful (*appositive, participial, relative clause*, and so on).

Sentence Play and Exploration

Students create or revise a few right-branching sentences in a current piece of writing. They can hand them in separately or highlight them when they submit the larger work. Coaching, of course, will be necessary, and students reflect on how the structures they created or revised strengthen the writing.

LESSON SET

CAN'T RESIST A LIST
The Compacting Power
of the Serial Comma

THE CONTEXT

In both fiction and nonfiction, writing is improved with concrete detail. Writers, in turn, need many strategies to pack examples or specific details into writing. Students compare two versions of the same information from George C. McGavin's *Smithsonian Handbooks: Insects* (2002). Both versions start with the same sentence because it sets a focus or context.

> Many people overlook the benefits that insects bring. Useful products are derived from insects. Honey and silk are derived from insects. Waxes are too. Oils are also derived from insects. In addition, natural medicines are derived from insects. Dyes are made from insects, too.

> *Many people overlook the benefits that insects bring. Useful products derived from insects range from honey and silk to waxes, oils, natural medicines, and dyes.*

Students react, sharing noticings, deciding which is most effective and why. Ask questions to deepen the conversation:

- Why do you think that?
- Show me where in the text you see that.
- How is this different/the same?

Discussion includes noticing the efficiency and economy of the second group of sentences. The elimination of repeated words and phrases is one way we make revision decisions. In revising this way, we create a series, and series of three or more items or actions are separated (and connected) with commas.

Lists are a fiction writer's friend as well. In *A Crooked Kind of Perfect*, author Linda Urban (2007) uses a list to emphasize the sheer number of "courses" Zoe's quirky father has taken in his Living Room University:

Already my dad has learned to Make Friends and Profit While Scrapbooking, Earn Bucks Driving Trucks, and Party Smarty: Turn Social Events into Cash Money.

THE POINTS OF EMPHASIS

- Commas and semicolons to separate items in a series
- Coordinating conjunctions
- Adjective order
- Prepositional phrases

THE DEMONSTRATION

To demonstrate the use of the serial comma as a strategy or option to revise, display the following simple sentences derived from Steve Jenkins's *The Beetle Book* (2012):

Beetles are found in many shapes.
Beetles are found in many sizes.
Beetles are also found in many colors.
There is an amazing range of shapes, sizes, and colors.
Beetles all share the same basic design.

When writers draft sentences, they later reread them to see if they need to revise them for clarity and flow. In the sentences that follow, we see a lot of repetition. Repetition can indicate that some words may be cut and the sentence revised. The repetition is underlined.

Beetles are found in many shapes.
Beetles are found in many sizes.
Beetles are also found in many colors.

Repetition can be wasteful. List lovers know a serial comma could help us revise these sentences. As a class, talk it out, then write it down.

Beetles are found in many shapes, sizes, and colors.

We don't need all of the information in the next sentence. We underline what we don't need.

There is an amazing range of shapes, sizes, and colors.

Now we delete the word *many* and replace it with the phrase *an amazing range of.*

Beetles are found in many shapes, sizes, and colors.

Beetles are found in *an amazing range of* shapes, sizes, and colors.

The next sentence seems to be saying something slightly different: *Beetles all share the same basic design.* The first sentence is about the *amazing range of shapes, sizes, and colors.* It focuses on the differences among beetles. This one is about how they are similar.

When we have two ideas opposing each other and we want to join them in one sentence, we can form a compound sentence. But in choosing which coordinating conjunction or FANBOYS (*for, and, nor, but, or, yet, so*) to use, we need to show that the second part is different from the first part. We could use words such as *but* or *yet* to show that difference.

Beetles are found in an amazing range of shapes, sizes, and colors, but beetles all share the same basic design.

Do we need to repeat the word beetle in the part of the sentence after the word *but*? We could say, *Beetles are found in an amazing range of shapes, sizes, and colors, but all share the same basic design.* Or we could use one of those stand-in words—or pronouns—for *beetles. Beetles* is plural, so we'd use *they.* We talk out the sentence in a couple of different versions and pick the one we like the best, selecting the word *all* to stand in for beetles rather than *they.*

Beetles are found in an amazing range of shapes, sizes, and colors, but all share the same basic design.

Now let's compare it with the author's original sentence—not because it's right, but because we want to see what revision decisions the author made.

Beetles are found in an amazing range of shapes, sizes, and colors, but they all share the same basic design.

Jenkins decided to refer to beetles by using the plural pronoun *they.* Both *all* and *they* work.

THE PRACTICE Students combine the following simple sentences with a partner. They are now trying on the role of revisers. We look at another sentence from Steve Jenkins's book on beetles.

Beetles are found in grasslands.
Beetles are found in forests.
Beetles are found in jungles.
Beetles are found in lakes and rivers.
Beetles are even found in deserts.

Beetles are not found in oceans.
Beetles are not found in polar regions.

Students use the Decisions Writers Make handout (see Appendix G) to revise the simple sentences in more than one way. Students share revisions, compare and contrast different responses, and then compare them with Jenkins's original, remembering we look only to see other options.

Except for the oceans and polar regions, beetles are found in almost every habitat: grasslands, forests, jungles, lakes and rivers—even deserts.

Tip

Colons and Dashes:—Oh, My!

Writers use colons and dashes in places that we often think of as slots for commas. If students are interested, teach them how to use a colon to introduce a list; it is fun for them, because it gives them an option in their writing they might not otherwise have. The use of a colon is shifting a bit now; students might see it used in published writing in a way that counters the traditional rule, which was to have a complete sentence before the colon and the list, as in Jenkins's example above. That is probably the safest use, but it is often used without a complete sentence in published writing. The rule is this: Does it work?

With the dash, it might be interesting to ask students about the difference in effect. Why use a dash when a comma would work? The dash connects like a comma, but with a different effect: the dash is less formal and also indicates a sudden break.

Students evaluate similarities and differences between their own versions and the author's and the effects created by the different options. We discuss their process, considering the following questions:

- What helped you most to revise the sentences?
- What are some patterns you noticed?
- Where would you use these patterns in your own writing? How would they help you as a writer?
- What questions do you still have?

THE COLLABORATION

Let's move on up the food chain and apply what we've learned to another living creature: lizards. Sneed B. Collard III (2012) says, "Lizards have some of the most robust appetites of any reptiles."

Groups of three to four revise their assigned cluster in at least two ways and then select and star their favorite.

2.1 The lizard menu stretches.
The menu stretches longer than a roll of toilet paper.
The roll of toilet paper is unraveled.

2.2 They dine on a variety of dishes.
The variety of dishes is wide.
The variety includes plant dishes and animal dishes.

2.3 Other lizards are vegetarian.
Vegetarians eat vegetation.
The vegetation they eat is mainly leaves.
The vegetation they eat is mainly flowers.
The vegetation they eat is mainly fruit.

2.4 However, it is a fact that is true that most other lizard species have a diet.
The diet is something they stick to.
The diet is lively.

2.5 Anoles are an example or instance.
Anoles provide pest-control services.
Their pest control services are top-notch.
They devour insects.

2.6 Other lizards eat almost anything that runs, crawls, flies, or breathes.
They eat birds.
They eat rodents.
They eat worms.
They eat deer.
They eat other reptiles.

Groups share their revised sentences, in order, one at a time, displaying them so that everyone can see them. Looking at the paragraph, students consider the sentences as part of a unit. Does the flow make sense? Do we need to add or rearrange anything?

Next, students compare their versions with the original paragraph from Sneed B. Collard III's *Most Fun Book Ever About Lizards*, not to correct their sentences or combinations, but to see the choices another author made. The class discusses how their sentences are like the author's. How are they different? What effects do the differences create?

The lizard menu stretches longer than an unraveled roll of toilet paper. Some lizards, such as the bearded dragon, are omnivores. They dine on a wide variety of plant and animal dishes. Other lizards, such as the common iguana, are vegetarian and eat mainly leaves, flowers, and fruit. However, most other lizard species stick to a lively diet. Anoles, for instance, provide top-notch pest-control services by devouring insects. Other lizards eat birds, rodents, worms, deer, other reptiles— almost anything that runs, crawls, flies, or breathes.

Tip | Oxford Comma Drama

Whether it's in the irreverent rock anthem by Vampire Weekend ("Oxford Comma") or a gristly grammar cop, people do care about that comma before the conjunction and last item in a series. It's called the Oxford comma because the Oxford University Press style guide advises using it for clarity. Otherwise you end up with a sentence like this: *For the special, BBC interviewed country singer George Jones's ex-wives, Johnny Cash and Kris Kristofferson.* Suddenly the sentence's intended meaning changes to one that is not intended. Because of the lack of the Oxford comma, Johnny Cash and Kris Kristofferson appear to be an appositive, renaming George Jones's ex-wives. Because of lack of clarity without the Oxford comma, *The Chicago Manual of Style, The Publication Manual of the American Psychological Association*, and the beloved *Elements of Style* by Strunk and White all recommend its use. On the other hand, the *Associated Press Stylebook*, used for journalistic writing, chooses not to use it unless a sentence contains a series of complex phrases because journalists make many decisions based on saving space. But writers also need to know that authors sometimes make a decision not to use our friend, the Oxford comma. For example, Laurel Snyder doesn't use it in *Bigger Than a Bread Box* (2011), to list some actions describing the main character's father (bold added):

*As far as I could tell, he was just **sitting on the couch, drinking a beer and watching TV**, like he usually does after dinner.*

In the end: You can be wrong without it, but you usually can't be wrong with it.

THE APPLICATION

Summarize and Serialize

After a lesson, read-aloud, or experience, partners write a sentence that includes a list to summarize or retell and that separates items with commas. For example, after reading the first section of *A Monster Calls* by Patrick Ness (2013), two students in a literature circle write the following:

The monster came in a dream, tried to threaten Conor, and didn't scare him.

Are You Serial?

Students return to previous writing and find a spot in which they used a general noun—words such as *stuff, things, stores,* or *places.* They circle it and replace it with a list of concrete nouns, being sure to use the serial comma correctly.

> *Original:* Marina had a lot of stuff on the floor of her room.
> *Revised:* Marina's bedroom floor was covered with socks, dishes, and every item of clothing she'd worn in the last two weeks.

Serially Prepared: List Maker

Students, using either one of the following situations or one like it, jot down a list of what they would need to prepare. Have them write their list of items as a sentence for someone who is going to help them, or as a wish list of supplies.

- Stranded on a desert island
- Seeing zombies attacking
- Getting lost on a mountain hike
- Cut off from town by a flood or landslide

Two eighth graders came up with this:

> If zombies are going to attack, you need running shoes (to run away from the slow moving threat), a shovel (to hit them over the head with), and an ax (to remove their heads to stop the zombie from regenerating).

Tip   Deleting Our Way to a Series

When we explain things, we don't want to repeat a sentence's subject over and over. Compare these two versions:

> The wind created a lot of destruction.
> The wind tore roofs off houses.
> The wind blew rocks into windows, breaking them.
> The wind knocked down power lines.

> The wind created a lot of destruction. It tore roofs off houses, knocked down power lines, and blew rocks into windows, breaking them.

Instead of repeating the subject, we use pronouns and list multiple verb phrases, separating those with commas. These constructions work well in informational writing and also aid writers in efficiently explaining a series of actions in a story or multiple causes or effects for an argument. Writers lean on the same principles of revising to avoid repetition of any element of a sentence: subjects, objects, or adjectives. Deleting extra words creates efficient and interesting writing.

LESSON SET

THE PAIR NECESSITIES
Balancing Pairs and Deleting Repetition

Head two columns with well-known pairs on a T-chart: *Bonnie and Clyde, Right or Wrong.* (See Figure L3.1.) Ask students what they notice, and discuss their responses. Beneath *Bonnie and Clyde,* add *Bert and Ernie* and *spaghetti and meatballs.* Ask students to help you add another item to the *Right-or-Wrong* column, such as *black or white.* Then partners add as many items to the columns as they can in two minutes, continuing the pattern.

Figure L3.1

Bonnie and Clyde	Right or Wrong
Spaghetti and meatballs Bert and Ernie	Black or white Day or night

After students share their lists, lead a discussion about the pattern: pairs, partnerships, and duos, with a coordinating conjunction (*and, or*) defining the relationship between the pairs. We consider the fact that pairs are as important as three-part lists and how—unlike lists—joining the two parts often doesn't require a comma (such as *plain and simple*). Instead, some sort of connector defines the relationship: conjunctions (*subordinate or coordinate*) or prepositions.

Display an excerpt from one of Mark Kurlansky's propositions in *World Without Fish* (2011):

> *It is important to understand that there are not two worlds: the world of humans and a separate world of plants and animals. There isn't a "natural world" and a "man-made world." We all live on the same planet and live in the same natural order.*

Students consider what they think Kurlansky is saying. If the word *argument* doesn't work its way into the discussion, explain that this entire expository book is a series of related arguments about saving the environment.

We study the excerpt, line by line:

It is important to understand that there are not two worlds.

Students reflect on how Kurlansky supports his claim in the sentences that follow it. Students begin to notice—eventually—that he uses pairs to argue that the world isn't a dichotomy of pairs: natural versus man-made. Bring the words *dichotomy, dual*, and *duet* into the discussion; it's the perfect time to review the prefixes *di-* and *du-* (meaning "two"):

There isn't a "natural world" and a "man-made world."

Students note the author's use of quotation marks to demonstrate the equalness or, in this case, the non-equalness of the terms, grouping and enclosing both with the marks.
Study the next line:

We all live on the same planet and live in the same natural order.

Students notice the word and phrase repetitions (*live on/in the same*) balancing the pair in this case.
Writers use pairs in the same way they use three-part lists—to pack more information into sentences—but in addition, pairs balance and pairs juxtapose, and the way we connect pairs defines the relationship between them. According to the *Oxford English Dictionary*, the word *balance* means "to estimate the two aspects or sides of anything, to ponder." I love the idea that the way we structure our sentences might cause our readers—or even the writer—to ponder. Writing is discovery, after all, and why wouldn't the structure of sentences continue to follow the path of our thinking, enhancing and clarifying, balancing and provoking thought?
Later, students analyze this excerpt from Malcolm Gladwell's *David and Goliath* (2013):

Wyatt Walker was a Baptist minister from Massachusetts. He joined up
with Martin Luther King in 1960. He was King's "nuts and bolts" man,
his organizer and fixer.

Students discuss how there are three simple sentences contained in the first sentence, and all the ways in which pairing pared them down to one.

Wyatt Walker was a minister.
Wyatt Walker was a Baptist.
Wyatt Walker was from Massachusetts.

Students build confidence as they become more conscious of how writers combine and pair ideas for efficient and clear sentences. When they see how we can avoid repetition by using pairs of subjects, objects, phrases, or adjectives, they understand a whole lot about how one revises sentences.

THE POINTS OF EMPHASIS

- Conjunctions
- Balance of pairs and parallelism
- Pairs versus lists
- Participial phrases
- Compound direct objects and verb phrases

THE DEMONSTRATION

These sentences from the book *Blizzard of Glass: The Halifax Explosion of 1917* by Sally Walker (2011) use multiple direct objects as a strategy to create efficiency in writing. The book tells the story of two ships colliding in the early 1900s, creating the largest man-made explosion in history until the nuclear bombs of World War II. The explosion nearly destroyed two cities. Display the following cluster of sentences:

> The shock wave snapped things.
> It snapped telegraph poles.
> It snapped trees in two.
> The snapping was easy.
> The snapping was as if the trees had been twigs.

Students reflect on what these sentences are communicating. After they identify the subject as the *shock wave*, they consider what the shock wave did, creating a basic sentence: *The shock wave snapped.* Our revision work helps us see how to add details to the main clause, expanding a basic sentence. We also discover that every time writers use a coordinating conjunction, they aren't necessarily creating a list. And when writers compose balanced pairs instead of lists, the pairs aren't separated by commas—still, a coordinating conjunction (FANBOYS: *for, and, nor, but, or, yet, so*) often defines the relationship of the pair.

Work with students to demonstrate the DRAFT strategies to combine the sentences (Appendix G).

> The shock wave easily snapped telegraph poles and trees in two.
> The shock wave snapped telegraph poles and trees in two easily.

We try a variety of constructions—a minimum of two. This requirement pushes flexibility and option shopping, which stretches writers to try new structures and allows for effective discussion. When students have more than one option, we discuss the differences in their effect. For example, students articulate the effect of the adverb placement in the sentence. In the first sentence, placing the adverb *easily* close to the verb seems to emphasize how easily the trees and telegraph poles snapped. Even though the second example seems to put the word *easily* in a spot of emphasis (the end of the sentence), it makes the snapping seem some how less significant.

Put Adverbs in Their Place

Generally, single-word adverbs work either before or after the verbs they modify. Proximity is a general rule of thumb. However, adverbs can be moved to places of emphasis (such as the end of the sentence), but only if they don't cause confusion there. Limiting modifiers (such as *only, just*, or *hardly*) should go *only just* before the word they modify.

Students grapple with how to include the last sentence of this cluster (*The snapping was as if the trees had been twigs*). The new idea makes a comparison: something is like something else. A couple of options exist for adding the comparison—using the clause to open or close the sentence: students like it after the base clause.

> The shock wave snapped telegraph poles and trees in two as easily as if they had been twigs.

Compare the class version to the original, not to match it, but to see what options Sally Walker chose:

> *The shock wave snapped telegraph poles and trees in two as easily as if they'd been twigs.*

There is only one small difference—the contraction of *they had*—and it probably resulted from the simple sentences we revised. This provides us with a chance to address formality in written language. See the Tip Box titled "Contraction Reaction."

One more thing students should notice about this sentence before moving on is how the compound objects were joined. Many students are confused about comma use, so use this sentence as a short refresher. Students identify the conjunction and what it is doing in the sentence, and then note the absence of a comma in this usage. Noticing that pairs of only two items don't require a comma prepares the groups for The Practice.

Contraction Reaction

Using contractions in speech is more common than using them in written texts. Because of that, contractions are often associated with informality, and the use of noncontracted verbs with more formal language. Some of that is true, but the level of formality is also a function of genre, audience, and purpose. Learning when it is appropriate to use contractions can be a helpful way for student writers to consider these important issues.

THE PRACTICE

Partners revise the following simple sentences, playing with language, talking out options. They may want to use the Decisions Writers Make handout (Appendix G).

> Electric wires were torn free.
> They were broken.
> They sizzled.
> They sparked.
> They were on the ground.

Partners revise the sentences in the cluster above in at least two different ways, starring their favorite. Students share starred revisions, comparing and contrasting different choices, discussing the different effects those choices create. Finally, they compare their creations with the author's original, remembering that the point is to consider the possible purposes for her choices—not to "correct" our constructions. We revisit the lack of commas in pairs. With so many verbs, the author chose to use them in sets of two— without commas—but two of them are in a slightly different form (as past participles) set off by commas. The depth of conversation depends on students' knowledge and preparation.

> Electric wires, **torn** free and **broken**, sizzled and sparked on the ground.
> Electric wires broke free, **sizzling** and **sparking** on the ground.

THE COLLABORATION

Each group receives one of the following sets of sentences. Groups revise them in at least two different ways, using the DRAFT strategies. Through students' messy talk, they revise, combining and deleting and making meaning.

3.1 Train cars toppled.
     They toppled off the rails.
     Wagons overturned.
     The horses that had pulled them lay dead.
     They were still in their harnesses.

3.2 The wave cracked things.
     It cracked the hulls of ships.

3.3 It smashed things.
     It smashed decks.
     The smashing came from flying debris.

3.4 Some things happened in Dartmouth.
     The rope factory was little more than a pile.
     The beer brewery was little more than a pile.
     The piles were of brick.

3.5 Some things happened throughout both cities.
     Windows were shattered.
     The windows were in homes.
     The windows were in stores.
     The windows were in offices.
     The windows were in schools.
     All of the shattered windows made a blizzard.
     The blizzard was of glass.
     The blizzard was deadly.

Once the class discusses their sentences, they combine them into a paragraph. When they are finished, they evaluate whether we need to add words or phrases, or rearrange ideas, to make the order seem smoother.

Compare and discuss Walker's original paragraph, not to correct but to explore the effects of choices:

> The shock wave snapped telegraph poles and trees in two as easily as if they'd been twigs. Electric wires, torn free and broken, sizzled and sparked on the ground. Train cars toppled off the rails, wagons overturned, and the horses that had pulled them lay dead in their harnesses. The wave cracked the hulls of ships and smashed the decks with flying debris. In Dartmouth, the rope factory and beer brewery were little more than piles of brick. Throughout both cities, the windows in homes and stores and offices and schools shattered in a deadly blizzard of glass.

Students evaluate similarities and differences between their own versions and the author's and the effects created by the different options. We discuss their process, considering the following questions:

- What helped you most to revise the sentences?
- What are some patterns you noticed?
- Where would you use these patterns in your own writing? How would they help you as a writer?
- What questions do you still have?

THE APPLICATION

A Pair of Friends, A Pair of Books

Partners turn to their independent reading and find at least two examples of sentences that use pairs (nouns, verbs, prepositions, participles, or any part of speech that is paired up to pare down). Show students an example from your own reading, such as this from Steve Sheinkin's *Bomb: The Race to Build—and Steal—the World's Most Dangerous Weapon* (2012; bold and italics added), which demonstrates a pair of prepositional phrases and participial phrases:

> *They starved* **through** *winter and* **into** *spring,* **dodging** *German patrols,* **waiting** *for their next job.*

This discussion expands the many ways in which writers can pair, as in this case, with prepositional and participial phrases. Both *through* and *into* head prepositional phrases joined by *and*. With both *dodging* and *waiting* in the *-ing* form, they are parallel. Balanced pairs put the *pare* into parallelism.

Revision Pairs: Pairing Up to Pare Down

Partners skim their writer's notebook for sentences that could be revised into one of the patterns of pairs we've observed. They find at least two places, revise the sentences, and then share them with a writing partner. Allison found these four sentences in her writer's notebook.

> I really like chatting with my friends on my cell phone. I also chat on my computer. We talk about what's going on in school. We also talk about homework.

She and her partner revised them in these two combinations. (Their favorite is starred.)

> * I really like chatting with my friends on my cell phone and computer, talking about what's going on at school and homework.

I really like chatting about school and homework with my friends—either on the computer or cell phone.

Writers share and discuss the different effects of their choices. After discussion, students write a quick note to themselves and answer this question: Do you like the original better or the revised one? Why?

Weather or Not: Observing Action

Watch a YouTube or other educational video of a natural disaster or event—something short with a lot of action. After viewing, partners each write five sentences about what they viewed. Partners revise two summaries into one, using parts of each person's writing and trying out a pattern of balance with pairs studied. Share the writing. (You may select the video or a choice of videos beforehand.)

One pair of students searched "cars sliding on ice video" and had many videos to choose from. This was the sentence they ended up with after going through the process:

An SUV started spinning and racing down the hill, out of control and unable to stop, slamming into a parked car, finally coming to a stop.

LESSON SET

4 ASIDES ARE EXTRA
Adding Flavor with Extra Information

When writing informational or explanatory texts, we often want to pack a lot into our sentences. What are our options?

Asides—or added bits of information—in sentences give readers the extra shot of clarification they need. Look at this paragraph from Nicola Davies's book *What's Eating You? Parasites—The Inside Story* (2009):

> *Human hair mites get all they need from their hosts—us. They are tiny relatives of spiders, about one-tenth of a millimeter long (smaller than a grain of salt), with bodies like miniature salamis and four pairs of stumpy legs. They live in the roots of hair (usually eyelashes or eyebrows), where they munch on dead skin and sebum (the oily stuff that keeps hair shiny). The only time they wander is when young mites search for a hair of their own, when they may find their way onto another body.*

As we study the paragraph, we note how Davies captures and communicates these asides of added information by using parentheses, commas, and dashes. These punctuation marks help writers communicate asides, or defining or clarifying information. We take apart each usage of those punctuation marks and discuss how they are used for asides. For example, the word *sebum* is defined in the parentheses that follow it: *sebum (the oily stuff that keeps hair shiny)*.

THE POINTS OF EMPHASIS

- Interrupter
- Nonrestrictive/parenthetical elements
- Transitional phrases
- Parentheses
- Adjective stacking (including hyphenated adjectives)
- Simple, compound, complex, and compound-complex sentences

THE DEMONSTRATION

To demonstrate the use of the interrupter pattern, compound sentences, and subordinate clauses as a strategy or option for revision, display the following cluster of simple sentences, based on Mary Roach's book *Gulp: Adventures on the Alimentary Canal* (2013):

> Cats can't taste sweetness.
> Dogs can taste sweetness.
> Other omnivores can taste sweetness.

After writers draft sentences, they reread them at some point later. Revising sentences makes them clearer, smoother, or more direct. These three sentences convey a lot of information. Since we want to find a way to revise these three sentences into one sentence that communicates the same ideas more efficiently, we reread and think. After reading the sentences, we get an idea: *Cats can't taste sweetness, but dogs and other omnivores can.* We talk it out.

> Cats can't taste sweetness, <u>while</u> dogs and other omnivores can.

We are able to revise the second two sentences into a **subordinate clause** to show the contrast to dogs and other omnivores. One student suggests we invert the sentences with the subordinate clause up front: *While cats can't taste sweetness, dogs and other omnivores can.* We decide it doesn't work as well because the main point of the sentence is about how cats differ from other omnivores; when we subordinate the cat side of the facts, the cats lose emphasis.

But we don't stop here. We try a few more ways. What about the interrupter pattern?

> Cats, unlike dogs and other omnivores, can't taste sweetness.

We keep talking sentences out, making revision decisions. Partners talk out the two options and decide which one they like better.

Is there another way? A compound sentence, maybe. Let's try.

> Cats can't taste sweetness, but dogs and other omnivores can.
> Cats can't taste sweetness; dogs and omnivores can.

Each group selects which sentence they like best and explains why; then they compare it with Mary Roach's original sentence to see how the author wrote it.

> *Cats, unlike dogs and other omnivores, can't taste sweetness.*

In this particular case, Mary Roach chose the interrupter pattern. Keeping the subject of the sentence up front helps retain its importance, but the idea of the contrast is emphasized by the interrupter prepositional phrase (beginning with *unlike*), showing contrast: *Cats,* **unlike dogs and other omnivores,** *can't taste sweetness.*

Here are more interrupter-pattern sentences, with the interrupters in bold, from Steve Jenkins's *Biggest, Strongest, Fastest* (1997):

The strongest animal, **for its size,** *is the ant.*

The Etruscan shrew, **the world's smallest mammal,** *could sleep in a teaspoon.*

Fortunately the snail, **with its hard shell,** *does not need to run away from danger.*

Tip Compound or Complex?

When students choose between complex and compound sentences, between subordinating ideas or joining whole sentences with *and* or *but*, they are really choosing how they want ideas to relate to each other. Compound sentences suggest an equal relationship between ideas, while subordination suggests a prioritizing one, the subordinate clause being less important than the main clause.

THE PRACTICE

With a partner, students combine the following sentence cluster based on ideas found in *Gulp!* To revise the sentences in more than one way, students may still benefit from using the sheet titled Decisions Writers Make (Appendix G).

Dry pet foods caught on during World War II.
The dry pet foods were cereal-based.
Tin-rationing put a stop to canning.
Tin-rationing included the canning of dog food.
The dog food was made from horse meat.
There was an abundance around the time Americans embraced the automobile.
They began selling their mounts to the knackers.

After they create at least two revisions, students star the combination they like best and share their favorites. We compare and contrast different responses, and finally compare their work with Mary Roach's original, reminding ourselves that we look only to see other options. If students need to make two sentences to make the writing clear, that's okay; the point is that they are honing, talking out, changing, removing, and replacing to get it as trim as they can.

> *Dry, cereal-based pet foods caught on during World War II, when tin-rationing put a stop to canning, including the canning of dog food made from horse meat (of which there was an abundance around the time Americans embraced the automobile and began selling their mounts to the knackers).*

Informational Text

Do you feel like your students lack experience with how to craft the syntax or flow of informational and explanatory writing? One way to help develop students' ear for sentence revising and style in informational writing is to read aloud nonfiction texts every day. Take a passage like this one from *Salt, Sugar, and Fat* by Michael Moss (2013) that has a subject similar to what you're currently discussing but that can be read aloud on its own.

The first thing you need to know about sugar is this: Our bodies are hard-wired for sweets.

Forget what we learned in school from that old diagram called the tongue map, the one that says our five main tastes are detected by five distinct parts of the tongue. That the back has a big zone for blasts of bitter and the sides grab the sour and salty, and the tip of the tongue has one single spot for sweet. The tongue map is wrong. As researchers would discover in the 1970s, its creators misinterpreted the work of a German graduate student that was published in 1901; his experiments showed only that we might taste a little more sweetness on the tip of the tongue. In truth, the entire mouth goes crazy for sugar, including the upper reaches known as the palate. There are special receptors for sweetness in every one of the mouth's ten thousand taste buds, and they are all hooked up, one way or another, to the parts of the brain known as the pleasure zones, where we get rewarded for stoking our body's energy. But our zeal doesn't stop there. Scientists are now finding taste receptors that light up for sugar all the way down our esophagus to our stomach and pancreas, and they appear to be intricately tied to our appetites.

The second thing to know about sugar: Food manufacturers are well aware of the food map folly, along with a whole lot more about why we crave sweets.

On another day, give students a copy of the text. To reinforce learning, students highlight one or more items from the list below to discuss:

- a convention or style choice that we've discussed before
- a convention or style choice that we haven't discussed
- any convention or style choice of interest

THE COLLABORATION

Groups of three or four revise sentence sets based on *Gulp!*, using the DRAFT strategies. Writers develop at least two different revisions, star the one they like best, and share their sentence and their rationale for selecting it.

4.1 Rodents are not like cats.
　　　Rodents are controlled by sweetness.
　　　Cats are not controlled by sweetness.
　　　One could say that rodents are slaves to sweetness.

4.2 Rats have been known to die.
　　　They die from not getting enough nutrition.
　　　A lack of nutrition is called malnutrition.
　　　Rather than step away from a drip of sugar water, rats die of malnutrition.

4.3 This was shown in a study.
　　　The study was about obesity.
　　　The study was from the 1970s.
　　　Rats were fed a supermarket diet.
　　　The diet was all you can eat.
　　　The diet included marshmallows.
　　　It also included milk chocolate and chocolate-chip cookies.
　　　The rats gained 269 percent more weight than rats fed standard laboratory fare.

(Option: As groups finish, give them this cluster as a challenge.)

4.4 There are strains of mice.
　　　Some strains will consume their own body weight.
　　　They will consume their body weight in diet soda.
　　　They will do this over the course of a day.
　　　You do not want the job of changing their bedding.

Groups share their favorite sentence one at a time, displaying them so everyone can see them. They combine them into a paragraph and then discuss, considering the following questions:

- Does the flow make sense?
- Do we need to reorder any sentences?
- Do we need to add or rearrange any parts of sentences to enhance flow or clarify meaning?

In this discussion, students begin to see that sentences relate to one another, that they carry meaning among and between them. Flow and variety matter, not simply individual sentence effectiveness.

Hyphenated Adjectives

Because Mary Roach's original paragraph contains three hyphenated adjectives, it may be a good idea to have students think about them ahead of time as a revising strategy. Generally, the rules for hyphenated adjectives are these:

- When two words join together to modify the same noun AND they come before the noun, they should be hyphenated, as in *best-selling novel* or *big-hearted moose* (Thidwick, from the book by Dr. Seuss).
- When a phrase works as a modifier, hyphenate it, as in *all-you-can-eat buffet* or *do-it-yourself book*.
- Do not hyphenate compound modifiers if the first word of the compound is *very* or an -ly word, as in *very big heart* or *freshly minted coin*.
- As a general rule of thumb, if the conjunction *and* could appear between adjectives, don't use a hyphen between them.

We compare the class paragraph with Mary Roach's, not to correct the students' revisions but to discuss the different effects created by Roach's decisions.

Rodents, on the other hand, are slaves to sweetness. They have been known to die of malnutrition rather than step away from a sugar-water drip. In an obesity study from the 1970s, rats fed an all-you-can-eat "supermarket" diet that included marshmallows, milk chocolate, and chocolate-chip cookies gained 269 percent more weight than rats fed standard laboratory fare. There are strains of mice that will, over the course of a day, consume their own body weight in diet soda, and you do not want the job of changing their bedding.

THE APPLICATION

One Food Sentence

Based on Hemingway's idea that a writer need only write "one true sentence" (Hemingway 1964), students write one food truth. With a partner, students write a true sentence about food or eating that demonstrates something they learned about sentences in these lessons. They may try an interrupter or hyphenated adjective in the sentence.

Deleting Eats the Unnecessary

Students return to a writer's notebook entry or draft and see what they can do about deleting words that don't do any work: unnecessarily repeated words, but also the trove of words that do nothing. If you can't stand the delete, get out of the kitchen. Will using parenthetical text or an aside help you eat some unnecessary verbiage?

In the Delete of the Night

Have a contest to see who can produce the best before-and-after sentence. The "after" sentence will have had words deleted and will be snappier and better. Using interrupters or asides can compact information and give readers sentence variety. Perhaps they revised a few sentences to make them better. Perhaps they rearranged a few chunks or added connector words such as subordinating conjunctions (*after, as, although, while, when, until, because, before, if, since*) or coordinating conjunctions (*for, and, nor, but, or, yet, so*). Perhaps they formed new verb endings. And we will know if they talked it out, because when we speak our sentences aloud, we make them stronger, tighter, and clearer.

LESSON SET

SENTENCES INTERRUPTED
The Power of Putting Ideas in the Way

When we speak, we often take little detours, adding commentary or additional information right in the middle of our sentences. Writers also provide these same detours to create interest, rhythm, emphasis, and variety. Compare these approaches to the same information:

> Fats Domino was another singer.
> He sang rock and roll.
> He put the sound of New Orleans in his music.

> *Fats Domino, another early rock & roll singer, put the sound of New Orleans in his music.*

Notice how the second sentence, from Holly George-Warren's *Shake, Rattle & Roll* (2001), has all the same ideas but arranges them in a way to show relationships and create interest. Writers also need to know that a common error is leaving off the second comma. The interrupter needs to be enclosed in commas or dashes.

We can do the same thing when we write, even if it's not a story we are writing. We can use these additions—ideas that interrupt the regular flow of the sentence—when we write information or argument. In all cases, the flow can add ideas that enhance the communication of our topic.

Teachers should keep a few facts in their back pockets. They may or may not surface in our discussions. Interrupters can be a word, a transition, a phrase, or a clause. This particular interrupter (*another early rock & roll singer*) is a **noun phrase**. This noun phrase, or **appositive**, is acting like a noun by renaming Fats Domino.

- Clauses, adverbial and relative
- Appositives and noun phrases
- Commas

Be Clause Minded

Clauses are groups of words that have both subjects and verbs in them, whereas phrases are groups of words without both subjects and verbs. Two types of clauses—*or modifiers*—are relative and adverbial clauses. **Relative clauses** act like **adjectives**, and **adverbial clauses** act like **adverbs**. Students may find it easier to think of these clauses as functioning like single-word modifiers.

Single-word adverbs answer the questions of *how, where, when*, and *to what extent: loudly, outside, yesterday, extremely*. So do **adverbial clauses**: *as though they were invisible* (how), *where the air is clear* (where), *after the bus had left* (when), *as fast as the others run* (to what extent).

Relative (or adjective) clauses do what single-word adjectives do. Adjectives answer *what kind* or *how many* or *which one*. Often they add details about nouns: *short* or *happy* or *blue*. Examples of relative clauses could include ***that*** *is made of chocolate*, ***who*** *rode the fastest*, ***which*** *they bought at the sale*.

THE DEMONSTRATION

The sentences for this lesson are derived from *On a Beam of Light*, a biography of Albert Einstein by Jennifer Berne (2013). Although the book is a biography, it focuses on the way Einstein noticed things and the way his noticings changed our world. Let's look at some sentences that are derived from that book. Display the following cluster of sentences:

Something happened over 100 years ago.
It happened as the stars swirled.
The stars swirled in the sky.
It happened as the Earth circled the sun.
It happened as the March winds blew.
The winds blew through a little town.
The little town was by a river.
The happening was that a baby boy was born.

After reading the complete cluster of sentences, students discuss what they notice about them. Among other observations, students note that readers don't find out what is actually happening until the last sentence in the cluster.

Sentence fluency is enhanced when writers vary the length of sentences. A short sentence after a long one can provide a nice "punch" to a sequence. In fact, Peter Roy Clark (2013) attributes this advice to Thomas Wolfe: "If you ever have a preposterous statement to make . . . say it in five words or less, because we're always used to five-word sentences as being the gospel truth." Because of that effect—drawing readers' attention—writers need to be careful to put the right kind of information in those short sentences. What do they want readers to pay attention to? What is the key information? That information might be perfect for a short sentence—but try it in a variety of ways to be sure.

Students decide to revise that cluster into three sentences. Here is what they settle on:

> Something happened over 100 years ago as the stars swirled in the sky. It happened as the Earth circled the sun and as the March winds blew through a little town by a river. A baby boy was born.

That sounds fine. But what do we notice? Repetition of the word *happened*. Is this effective or not?

The Truth About Repetition

There is no such thing as repetition. Only insistence.

—Gertrude Stein

Young writers often hear the advice to avoid repetitions. It's true that using repeated filler words isn't effective. It's true that mindlessly repeating isn't effective, either. But sometimes choosing important words and repeating them in key places can be effective. Look at this passage from *Rosa* by Nikki Giovanni (2005; bold added):

> She sighed as she realized she was **tired**. Not **tired** from work but **tired** of putting white people first. **Tired** of stepping off sidewalks to let white people pass, **tired** of eating at separate lunch counters and learning at separate schools. She was **tired** of "Colored" entrances, "Colored" balconies, "Colored" drinking fountains, and "Colored" taxis. She was **tired** of getting somewhere first and being waited on last. **Tired** of "separate," and definitely **tired** of "not equal."

How many times does Giovanni use the word *tired*? What other words are repeated? (*White, separate, colored.*) Is the repetition effective? Writers may use repetition as a default, failing to seek a precise word. But effective repetition, as we can see in the *Rosa* paragraph, helps create rhythm and balance, emphasis and effect, unity and order.

Thinking of our DRAFT strategies, what might we delete in these sentences? We decide to delete one of the two uses of *happened.*

Something happened over 100 years ago as the stars swirled in the sky, as the Earth circled the sun, and as the March winds blew through a little town by a river. A baby boy was born.

Let's not forget that the adverbial clauses—beginning with *as* and telling a series of things that are happening—need to be separated by commas since there are more than two of them. Let's look at Berne's version and see what choices she made:

Over 100 years ago, as the stars swirled in the sky, as the Earth circled the sun, and as the March winds blew through a little town by the river, a baby boy was born.

Some students mourn the loss of the short sentence they had selected in their revision. Interestingly, the next sentence in the book IS short: "His parents named him Albert." When students consider this, they see the effect of the short sentence following a long one. In the class's version, the focus on the event of the birth is clear. In the book, the short sentence focuses our attention on the name of the baby.

THE PRACTICE

Students grapple with the following sentence cluster with a partner, making revision decisions about how to combine them:

One day something happened.
It happened when Albert was sick.
He was sick in bed.
The happening was that his father brought him something.
It was a compass.
A compass was a small case.
It was a round case.
Inside was a magnetic needle.

Student partnerships revise the sentences in the cluster above in at least two different ways, starring their favorite. Then they share revisions, comparing and contrasting their different choices and discussing the different effects those choices create. For support in making revision decisions, students may use Appendix G.

Appositives: Interrupter Classic

Appositives, *nouns or noun phrases that go right next to nouns or ideas they modify,* are quite useful to writers. Appositives give explanatory information efficiently. They add additional—although not necessarily essential—information and are usually set off by a comma or commas, although they can be set off by a dash or dashes. It is also important to note that not all appositives are interrupters. This example from Jennifer Berne does not interrupt the sentence, but it is an appositive, or noun phrase, renaming the noun before it (bold added):

> *One day, when Albert was sick in bed, his father brought him a compass—**a small round case with a magnetic needle inside**.*

Next, students compare their responses to the author's original, with a focus on considering possible purposes for choices—not to "correct" our constructions.

> *One day, when Albert was sick in bed, his father brought him a compass—a small round case with a magnetic needle inside.*

Unless students have already discussed the use of dashes as a way to punctuate interrupters, this would be a good time to have a short lesson on the choice of punctuation for interrupters: commas, dashes, or parentheses. Each one has a slightly different effect—and some writing situations are more likely to use one over another. This might also be a good time to mention the placement of interrupters. If it's appropriate, teachers could pause for a short lesson on misplaced modifiers, just to help students understand how placement of phrases and clauses matters in terms of clear communication of meaning. For instance, in *The Port Chicago 50* (2014), Steve Sheinkin decided on this final sentence (bold added):

> *A six-foot-three, 225-pound Texan, Miller was the ship's heavyweight boxing champ.*

Look at the effects that moving words around has on the clarity or meaning.

> Miller was the ship's heavyweight boxing champ, **a six-foot-three, 225-pound Texan**.

> Miller, **a six-foot-three, 225-pound Texan**, was the ship's heavyweight boxing champ.

THE COLLABORATION   In small groups or pairs, students revise one of the following sets of sentences from Berne's *On a Beam of Light* (2013). Revising the sentences in at least two different ways, groups choose one to share.

5.1 Something didn't matter.
It didn't matter which way Albert turned the compass.
The needle always pointed north.
It was as if it were held.
The holding was by an invisible hand.

5.2 Albert was so amazed.
His amazement made his body tremble.

5.3 Suddenly he knew something.
He knew there were mysteries.
The mysteries were in the world.
The mysteries were hidden.
The mysteries were silent.
The mysteries were unknown.
The mysteries were unseen.

5.4 He wanted something.
He wanted it more than anything.
He wanted to understand those mysteries.

Once the class discusses their sentence creations, they arrange them into a paragraph. In this sequence, it's possible that some sentences do not have interrupters. Even though this lesson focuses on them, it's important for students to understand that not every sentence will (or should) have them. What would it sound like if they all did?

Students compare the class draft with Berne's version, not for correction but for exposure to other options and their effects. Here is the original paragraph:

One day, when Albert was sick in bed, his father brought him a compass—a small round case with a magnetic needle inside. No matter which way Albert turned the compass, the needle always pointed north, as if held by an invisible hand. Albert was so amazed his body trembled. Suddenly he knew there were mysteries in the world—hidden and silent, unknown and unseen. He wanted, more than anything, to understand those mysteries.

Students evaluate similarities and differences between their own versions and Berne's, discussing the effects created by the different options. We discuss their revision decisions and reflect on the following questions:

- What helped you most to revise the sentences?
- What are some patterns you noticed?
- Where would you use these patterns in your own writing? How would they help you as a writer?
- What questions do you still have?

THE APPLICATION

Excuse Me!

Students turn to their individual reading and find at least two sentences that use interrupters to add detail and variety to the sentence structures. In small groups, students share examples and categorize them. Students draw some conclusions about interrupters (placement, purpose, punctuation) and create a chart about them to share with the class. Here is an example:

Figure L5.1

What We Discovered About Interrupters in Loree Griffin Burns's *Tracking Trash* (2007)	
Examples from the Text to Think About (bold added)	
Ships sailing from Europe to America, **on the other hand**, could be delayed for weeks if they tried to sail against the stream's flow. Scientists believe the warm waters of the Gulf Stream heat the winds that, **in turn**, carry a pleasant climate to Northern Europe.	Modern ocean scientists, **or oceanographers**, call these streams "currents," and we know that they affect our world in ways that go far beyond the sailing of ships. These changes, **which can include depleted fish populations and increased rainfall**, have a large impact on the lives and livelihoods of people who live in the area.
Our Thinking—if you interrupt, you're going to need two commas.	
Sometimes interrupters are transitions.	Interrupters can rename or give more information. They aren't all the same, except they interrupt.

May I Interrupt Here?

Students scour drafts in their writer's notebooks to find places in their writing that could be enhanced by an interrupter or that could benefit from more detail. They should consider the punctuation as an effect along with the interrupter: commas, dashes, or parentheses? After they write at least two different sentences with interrupters, they should work with a partner to see if the revised sentences are effective and to explain the choice of punctuation. **Here are some examples:**

> *Original:* My sister is an irritation magician. She can magically invent new ways to irritate me with the swish of a wand, which in her case is a large pink pencil Meemaw got her at the flea market.

> *Revised:* My sister, **the irritation magician**, is constantly performing new tricks . . . to irritate me. With the swish of a wand—**in her case an enormous pink pencil from the flea market**—she abracadabras new ways to torture me.

Do You Mind If I Say Something?

Students find a passage of about 100 words in a book or article they enjoy. They rewrite a few lines of their passage by adding two or three interrupters to reflect a character thinking or the personality of the author, to add interesting information, or to address the audience. Revisers share both versions with a partner. Then partners discuss the differences and the effects: Is the revision better? Worse? Why?

Here is an example of a few sentences a pair of seventh graders revised from *The Zombie Survival Guide* by Max Brooks (2003).

> Although their vocal cords are capable of speech, their brain—**what there is of it**—is not.

> This moan—**MMMMMM**—is released when zombies identify prey.

> It will then shift in tone—**more frantic**—and volume—**louder**—as the zombie commences its attack.

The Long and the Short of It

To reinforce our initial look at sentence-length variety, students look in the texts they read for long and short sentences in proximity—sentences that are neighbors, if you will, but not necessarily next-door neighbors. The longer sentences can be with or without commas.

Here are two long-and-short pairs found in Laurie Halse Anderson's *Chains* (2008):

> Long: *We couldn't take Momma's shells, nor Ruth's baby doll made of flannel bits and calico, nor the wooden bowl Poppa made for me.*

> Short: *Nothing belonged to us.*

Long: *I looked around our small room, searching for a tiny piece of home I could hide in my pocket.*

Two short: *What to take?*

　　　Seeds.
(The two short sentences are even two separate paragraphs.)

Students reread the long and short sentences they found. They consider the effects of the closeness of the long and the short sentences. Why do writers craft these different sentences? What are the effects of short and long sentences? What do they do together?

Students write a few sentences of reflection on these questions below their collected sentences, making sure to show a connection to the sentences collected.

The Long (or Short) Shot
In their writer's notebook entry or an essay they're working on or have completed, students experiment with something they've discovered about long and short sentences. They should highlight and label the work "The Long and the Short of It." Then they describe what they did and why in a sentence or two. (The changing and adding may be done on a sticky note and attached to the work if students want to preserve their original.)

LESSON SET

THE PARTICIPLE PRINCIPLE

The Verbal That Tracks Action

Writers sometimes need to add detail or explanation to make their points clear. They can do so in a variety of ways. Let's look at one, with sentences based on Adina Rishe Gerwitz's *Zebra Forest* (2013):

> The man stood very still.
> The man was looking at us.
> The man tried to focus his eyes in the sudden light.

Often we think of lists as ways to compact writing, but there is another easy-to-use tool to layer ideas economically: the participle.

> The man stood very still.
> The man was **looking** at us.
> The man tried to focus his eyes in the sudden light.

We could easily revise the first two sentences using the participle to head a participial phrase:

> The man stood very still, **looking at us**.

Looking at us is a participial phrase. The *-ing* verb, for short, at the beginning is a participle.

What about adding the third sentence to our new one? If we change the verb *tried* to *trying*, we could attach that as well. That's what Gerwitz did in *Zebra Forest*:

> *The man stood there very still, **looking** at us, **trying** to focus his eyes in the sudden light.* (bold added)

Writers contrast this with the three sentences we started with. Beyond lists, participial phrases are compact ways to add information and action or motion to the end, middle, or beginning of sentences.

- Participial phrases
- Introductory prepositional phrases
- Relative pronouns and clauses
- Introductory adverbial clauses (adjectives)

Students work with sentences from Jim Arnosky's book *Wild Tracks!* (2008). The book explores animal tracks and how people learn about animals from them.

Display the following cluster of sentences:

Bears walk.
They walk flat-footed.
Flat footed means placing the foot on the ground.
It is the entire foot.
This happens with each step.

We consider what we notice about these sentences. Students observe that the sentences seem very straightforward: something happens (bears walk flat-footed), and this is what *flat-footed* means. Together, we use the DRAFT strategies (Appendix G) to analyze the sentence cluster to see what might be deleted or rearranged. Do we need to add connectors or form new verb endings? To make our revision decisions, we talk it out.

If we combine the first two sentences in this cluster, we can delete *they* as a repetition of *bears*.

Bears walk flat-footed.

Students notice that the last three sentences define what flat-footed means. They create a new sentence with the last three sentences of the cluster. Students consider how to add the new information to the sentence.

They could use a *which means* phrase or even add a participle like *placing*—the action the foot takes. After looking at both options, students pick this:

Bears walk flat-footed, **placing** the entire foot fully on the ground with each step.

Compare students' revisions with Arnosky's to see what options the author chose:

> *Bears walk flat-footed, placing the entire foot on the ground with each step.*

THE PRACTICE

Student partners revise the following cluster of sentences in two different ways and choose their favorite. Students may use the handout Decisions Writers Make (Appendix G).

> The front feet are wide.
> They show in bear tracks.
> They show completely.
> The hind feet are large.
> They show in bear tracks.
> They show completely.

After students share their favorites and discuss the differences and the effects of those differences, compare their revisions with Arnosky's, again just to see the effects of different choices:

> *The wide front feet and the large hind feet show completely in bear tracks.*

Tip Adjectives In and Out of Place

Adjectives in English sentences are usually placed just before the nouns they modify. However, your students may be familiar with the stylistic device of putting adjectives *out* of their expected place, either from their own reading or from having worked with Harry Noden's *Image Grammar* (2012). If they are, they may have revised with the focus on the adjectives by putting them in places of emphasis or out of their "normal" positions. Their sentences may look something like this: *The bear's front feet, wide, and the hind feet, large, show completely in tracks.* Or this: *The bear's feet—large and wide—show completely in tracks.* Although both of these could work and reflect interesting literary style, teachers might want students to consider why, in this instance, the author chose to use the adjectives in the expected positions. Part of that choice may have to do with context.

THE COLLABORATION

In partners or small groups, students revise an assigned set of sentences in at least two different ways and select one to share with the class.

6.1 The front feet show up.
They show up in the tracks.
The front portion of the hind feet show up.
They show up in the tracks.
They show up when the bear is running.

6.2 A bear is a heavy animal.
The heaviness makes something happen.
Its tracks are pressed.
They are pressed deeply.
They are pressed often.
They create defined footprints.
The definition is perfect.

6.3 An experienced tracker can estimate.
A tracker uses a set of footprints.
A perfect set of footprints is two front and two hind.
A tracker can estimate the size of the bear.
The size is the size of the one that made the tracks.
A tracker can estimate the weight of the bear.

6.4 A bear's toes spread apart.
They do this on slippery surfaces.
They do it for better traction.
The spreading presses footprints.
The footprints are large.
They are larger than the bear's actual feet.

After sharing, students combine each group's sentence into a paragraph; following the order of the second number will put the paragraph in the order of the author. Then they can compare their paragraph with the passage from *Wild Tracks!* (2008), highlighting different choices and discussing their effects.

> *Bears walk flat-footed, placing the entire foot on the ground with each step. The wide front feet and the large hind feet show completely in bear tracks. When running, the front feet and the front portion of the hind feet show up in the tracks. Because a bear is a heavy animal, its tracks are often pressed deeply, creating perfectly defined footprints. With a perfect set of four bear footprints (two front and two hind), an experienced animal tracker is able to accurately estimate the size and weight of the bear that made them. On slippery surfaces, a bear's toes spread apart for better traction, pressing in footprints that are much larger than the bear's feet. Such splayed footprints can fool a tracker into imagining the bear that left them is much larger than its actual size.*

Students evaluate similarities and differences between their own versions and the author's and the effects created by the different options. We discuss their process, considering the following questions:

- What helped you most to revise the sentences?
- What are some patterns you noticed?
- Where would you use these patterns in your own writing? How would they help you as a writer?
- What questions do you still have?

THE APPLICATION

Tracking the Action

Harry Noden explains that "participles evoke action," and that "using single participles creates rapid movement, while expanded phrases add details at a slower, but equally intense pace" (2011, 4–5). To see this effect, students read the following passage from the first chapter of *Where the Red Fern Grows* (Rawls 1961), without the participles and participial phrases:

> *I was trying to make up my mind to help when I got a surprise. Up out of that mass reared an old redbone hound. For a second I saw him. I caught my breath. I couldn't believe what I had seen.*
>
> *He fought his way through the pack and backed up under the low branches of a hedge. They formed a halfmoon circle around him. A big bird dog, bolder than the others, darted in. The hedge shook as he tangled with the hound. He came out so fast he fell over backwards. I saw that his right ear was split wide open. It was too much for him and he took off down the street.*
>
> *A big ugly cur tried his luck. He didn't get off so easy. He came out with his left shoulder laid open to the bone. He sat down on his rear and let the world know that he had been hurt.*
>
> *By this time, my blood was boiling. It's hard for a man to stand and watch an old hound fight against such odds, especially if that man has memories in his heart like I had in mine. I had seen the time when an old hound like that had given his life so that I might live.*
>
> *I waded in.*

Students share what they can see and hear in the passage. Most of the time, they have some answers, but they don't have as many as they do when they read the original passage, which follows. The participles and participial phrases are in bold for ease in identification.

> *I was trying to make up my mind to help when I got a surprise. Up out of that **snarling, growling, slashing** mass reared an old redbone hound. For a second I saw him. I caught my breath. I couldn't believe what I had seen.*

Twisting and slashing, he fought his way through the pack and backed up under the low branches of a hedge. Growling and snarling, they formed a halfmoon circle around him. A big bird dog, bolder than the others, darted in. The hedge shook as he tangled with the hound. He came out so fast he fell over backwards. I saw that his right ear was split wide open. It was too much for him and he took off down the street, squalling like a scalded cat.

A big ugly cur tried his luck. He didn't get off so easy. He came out with his left shoulder laid open to the bone. He sat down on his rear and let the world know that he had been hurt.

By this time, my fighting blood was boiling. It's hard for a man to stand and watch an old hound fight against such odds, especially if that man has memories in his heart like I had in mine. I had seen the time when an old hound like that had given his life so that I might live.

Taking off my coat, I waded in.

With the participles added, students consider what they see and hear. They note that in addition to adding sensory details, the participles—those *-ing* words that we deleted in the first version—actually add to the intensity and ferocity of the fight. The words themselves, their meanings and their sounds, help to create the action and movement of the fight: *twisting and slashing, growling and snarling.*

Making Tracks

Students look for examples of long and short participial phrases (or single-word participles) in their reading. They collect three or four of them and share them in small groups where they can make a list of noticings about the placement and effects of participial phrases. Their lists can be compiled to create a class chart of Dos and Don'ts About Participial Phrases, like these three initial items they may develop:

1. *Do* use participial phrases to create more action in a passage.
2. *Do* make sure the phrases are close to the word they are describing to avoid confusion.
3. *Don't* think that EVERY word that ends in *-ing* is a participle.

Hunting, Tracking, and Identifying Participles

Students look in their writer's notebook for a passage they have drafted that could use more detail or action. They highlight any existing participial phrases and then find places to add a few more. With a writing partner, they compare each before-and-after version to get feedback on the effectiveness of their revisions.

LESSON SET

7

A VERBAL REMEDY
Invigorating Writing with Gerunds and Participles

The truth about gerunds and participles is this: How you use them is more important than what you call them. Writers use verbs in different ways as one means of creating lively, concise writing. We can use verbs like nouns (gerunds) or adjectives (participles). For example, in the sentences *I love revising* and *Revising is fun*, the verb *revising* functions as a noun (an activity). That's a **gerund**.

On the other hand, if I say, *I talk out my sentences, revising as I go*, the word *revising* is a **participle**, heading a **participial phrase**, which functions as an adjective. Grammarians would say it's adjectival. Does that matter? Perhaps it feels more like verbal abuse. But at least you know a bit more about verbs that end in *-ing.**

Students compare the following, which summarize the setting of the book *Bomb: The Race to Build—and Steal—the World's Most Dangerous Weapon* by Steve Sheinkin (2012):

> Scientists in the late 1930s engaged in a frantic race. They were breaking atoms and working in secret facilities because they were trying to gain world dominance.

> Scientists in the late 1930s engaged in a frantic race, breaking atoms, working in secret facilities, trying to gain world dominance.

Ask follow-up questions to deepen the conversation:

- Why do you think that?
- Where in the text do you see that?
- What construction creates that effect?

---

*Whereas *present* **participles** do end in *-ing*, *past* **participles** end in *-ed* or *-en.*

Discussion includes noticing that the first brief summary of *Bomb* gets at the main idea behind the book—spies and secrets—but doesn't capture the mood very well. The use of verbals in the second draft increases the pace and intensity—just like the mood of the time.

THE POINTS OF EMPHASIS

- Gerunds (verbals)
- Prepositional phrases
- Participial phrases (verbals)
- Noun clauses
- Adverbial clauses
- Commas in series
- Dashes
- Transitions

THE DEMONSTRATION

To demonstrate the way in which participial phrases add interest and information, display the following cluster of sentences derived from Deborah Heiligman's award-winning book, *Charles and Emma: The Darwins' Leap of Faith* (2009).

> Charles could do something.
> He could entertain himself.
> He could do it for hours.
> He did it just by thinking.
> He did it just by observing birds.
> He did it just by watching sticks.
> He did it just by watching leaves.
> He watched sticks and leaves float.
> They floated down a stream.

DRAFT reminds us to *delete* words that are repeated, unless the repetition serves a purpose of emphasis or rhythm. Ask students what could be deleted in the first sentences.

> Charles <u>could</u> entertain himself.
> He <u>could</u> do it for hours.

Deleting the second *could* revises the sentence like this:

> Charles could entertain himself for hours.

The next four sentences also have unnecessary repetition:

He did it just by thinking.
He did it just by observing birds.
He did it just by watching sticks.
He did it just by watching leaves.

How do these ideas relate to the idea we already have? Since they are ways in which he entertained himself, how can we add them to our sentence? Students remember that lists use commas to separate individual items.

Charles could entertain himself for hours just by thinking, by observing birds, by watching sticks, and by watching leaves.

Students might note that they could also delete the word *by* from some of the phrases. Actually, they could eliminate the word entirely by using a series of gerunds instead of the bulkier prepositional phrases that start with *by*.

Charles could entertain himself for hours, just thinking, observing birds, and watching sticks and leaves.

Tip Is It a Gerund? Or Something Else?

Gerunds are words that look like -*ing* verbs but act like nouns. Since gerunds function as nouns, they can be the subjects of sentences as well as objects of verbs or prepositions. A way to think about the difference is to consider this question: What are your hobbies? Reading? Skiing? Scuba diving? Running? Writing? These are things we do (verbs); however, they are also names of activities (nouns) when used in this way. I love running. *Running* is a gerund (in this sentence too).

Students discuss options for the last two sentences. How do they relate to what we have already? Writers notice that these sentences add details to the last items on our list—what Charles is watching.

Charles could entertain himself for hours, just thinking, observing birds, and watching sticks and leaves float down a stream.

Let's look at the original to see what options the author chose:

Charles could entertain himself for hours just by thinking, or by observing birds, or watching sticks and leaves float down a stream.

Students will note, in comparing their revisions with the original, that the author chooses to keep some of the prepositions and uses the conjunction *or* instead of *and*. Address the different effects each of those have on the sentence.

THE PRACTICE

Students tangle with the following cluster of sentences with a partner, revising them in at least two different ways and starring the one they like best. Evaluation is a big part of revision decisions. For supporting their revision decisions, students may use the DRAFT handout (Appendix G).

> He made notes.
> He did this as he watched.
> He watched the birds.
> He wrote.
> He wrote what the birds did.
> He wrote how they behaved.

When students finish revising the sentences, they share their favorite revisions. After sharing, they compare their creations to the original, not to correct their work but to see how different revision decisions create different effects. Out of all the possibilities, why did the author choose the one she did? Ask the students, "Do you agree or disagree? Why?"

> *He made notes as he watched the birds, writing down what they did, how they behaved.*

Participles . . . *Whuh?*

If students have worked with participles before, this cluster of sentences provides a good time to review and extend. *He made notes as he watched the birds, writing down what they did, how they behaved.* In this case, the subject (Charles) has a main action of making notes. Students could see the second verb, *writing*, as separate. In actuality, *writing* is a description of his note making, modifying the kind of notes he made, spiraling back to the base clause. By the way, when we refer to *a* participle, we use the word *participle*. On the other hand, when we refer to a phrase in which the first word is a participle, we can call it a *participial phrase* or a *participle phrase*.

THE COLLABORATION

Assign small groups different sentence sets. Groups revise their assigned sentences in at least two ways and then select their best one.

7.1 And he was like many.
   He was like young boys.
   He was a collector.

7.2 He collected things.
   He collected shells.
   He collected seals.
   He collected coins.
   He collected minerals.

7.3 He studied what he collected.
   He organized them by kind.
   His organization was in a tradition.
   The tradition was of natural historians.

7.4 His great love was hunting.
   Another great love was shooting.
   These loves came as he got older.

7.5 He shuddered.
   He shuddered later in life.
   He shuddered at something.
   The something was how many animals he had killed.

7.6 He quivered.
   He quivered with joy.
   He quivered with excitement.
   His quivering was before picking up a gun.
   His quivering was at the time of his youth.

Groups share their favorite revisions, recording them so other students can see them. As students compile the sentences into a paragraph, they might want to talk about connectors. How can they make the flow of sentences work?

Helping students work through the process, with the specific consideration of transitions, should be helpful to them. After they have resolved the challenge, have them consider Heiligman's original paragraph from *Charles and Emma*, here with some transitions underlined. What differences do they notice? How can what they observe help them in their own writing when they need to move back and forth through time?

Charles could entertain himself for hours just by thinking, or by observing birds, or watching sticks and leaves float down a stream. He *made notes as he watched the birds, writing down what they did, how they behaved. And like many young boys, he was a collector. <u>He</u> collected shells, seals, coins, and minerals. <u>He</u> studied them and organized them by kind—in the tradition of natural historians. <u>As he got older</u>, his great love was hunting and shooting. <u>Later in life</u> he shuddered at how many animals he had killed. <u>But at the time</u> he quivered with joy and excitement before picking up a gun.*

Connectors

Connectors are words or phrases that help readers see the relationships among and between sentences. Sometimes they are straightforward and fairly simple (*first, on the other hand, yet, after*), but other times they are more sophisticated and subtle. Notice the bold words in the following passage as examples of ways in which Laura Hillenbrand (2001) uses connectors to link ideas in this paragraph from *Seabiscuit: An American Legend*. She uses pronouns and synonyms to show relationships between one example and another.

> *The only thing more dangerous than being on the back of a racehorse was **being thrown** from one. <u>Some</u> jockeys took two hundred or more **falls** in <u>their</u> careers. **Some** were **shot into the air** when horses would "prop," or plant <u>their</u> front hooves and slow abruptly. <u>Others</u> **went down** when <u>their</u> mounts would bolt, **crashing into the rails** or even the grandstand. A common accident was "clipping heels," in which trailing horses tripped over leading horses' hind hooves, usually sending the trailing horse and rider into a **somersault**. Finally, horses could break down, racing's euphemism for incurring leg injuries.*

Obvious Connectors	Subtle Connectors
Transition Words: *or, when, and, finally, which*	Synonyms: *being thrown, falls, shot in the air, went down, crashing into the rails, somersault*
Prepositions: *on, of, from, in, over, into*	Pronouns: *some, their, others*

THE APPLICATION

Observation Station

Pull several powerful paragraphs, plump with transitions, from texts, and make copies of them. Set up a station where students can stop by and highlight those phrases and words that help connect ideas in the paragraphs.

Perhaps put a copy of Charting Connections (Appendix F) at the table to help in this endeavor. Students contribute to a chart about how transitions could work. Here is a contribution one student made:

A pronoun can connect because it stands in for a noun we've already used.

Be a Sentence Scientist

Students find a few sentences that use gerunds or participles. In pairs, students rewrite the sentences without the verbals. The following sentences are from *The Tin Forest* by Helen Ward (2001):

Small creatures appeared, creeping among the forest of trees.

Revision:

Small creatures appeared; they seemed to creep among the forest of trees.

Soon the song of birds mingled with the buzzing of insects and the rustle of leaves.

Revision:

Soon the song of birds mingled with the sounds of insects and leaves.

Writer's Advice Column

After collecting and rewriting sentences with participles and gerunds, students discuss the different effects with a partner. Then they each write a few advice statements for others, like this example:

Dear Trying Writing in Detroit,

Participles or gerunds can help you say what you want to say faster. Gerunding is fun, but participles, taking a bit longer, are the most fun.

Sincerely,
Crushing Grammar

LESSON SET

8 KEEP YOUR READER ORIENTED

Using Prepositions to Connect and Navigate

THE CONTEXT

Readers need to see the settings writers describe, the places where characters or people dwell. One essential tool for locating your reader in time and space is the preposition. Students compare these two versions of the same idea, based on L. D. Harkrader's *Airball: My Life in Briefs* (2008):

> I just stood there, clutching the basketball tightly. A wild October wind whipped, rattling the windows.

> *I just stood there on the free-throw line, in the shadow of that big orange sign above the scoreboard, clutching the basketball tight to my chest. Outside, a wild October wind whipped through town, rattling the windows high above the bleachers in the gym.*

Prepositions clarify the relationships between and among words, defining location or position as well as other kinds of relationships.

Alphabetical List of Common Prepositions					
about	before	except	near	than	with
above	behind	excluding		through	within
across	below		of	throughout	without
after	beneath	following	off	to	
against	beside	for	on	toward	
along	between	from	onto		
among	beyond		out	under	
around	by	in	outside	underneath	
at		inside	over	unlike	
atop	down	into		until	
	during		past	up	
			per	upon	

As students respond with comparisons and differences, they underline the prepositional phrases and highlight the prepositions (in bold) that begin the phrases in the original, more descriptive passage from Harkrader's book and discuss the relationships reflected by the prepositions.

*I just stood there **on the free-throw line**, **in the shadow** **of that big orange sign** **above the scoreboard**, clutching the basketball tight **to my chest**. Outside, a wild October wind whipped **through town**, rattling the windows high **above the bleachers** **in the gym**.*

Discuss how writers use prepositional phrases to ground readers in time and space.

THE POINTS OF EMPHASIS

- Prepositional phrases
- Participles
- Conjunctions

THE DEMONSTRATION

To demonstrate that prepositions are often about location, display the following complete sentences about a specific place in *Liar & Spy*, by Rebecca Stead (2013):

It's a tiny little room.
It's almost a closet.
The room has walls that are dingy.
The room has a floor that is concrete.
The room has one lightbulb.
The lightbulb dangles from the ceiling.
The lightbulb dangles in a way that's slightly creepy.

The DRAFT mnemonic (Appendix G) reminds us of some strategies we might use to revise these sentences into one sentence. First, delete information that's redundant or repetitive.

It's a tiny little room.
<u>It's</u> almost a closet.

Repetition of this type is wasteful. Here a punctuation connector can help us revise. Talk it out and write down some options.

It's a tiny little room, almost a closet.

The next three sentences start with *the room has*, so there are some more words to delete.

> The room has walls that are dingy.
> The room has a floor that is concrete.
> The room has one lightbulb.

We already have the word *room*, so we could delete these repetitions and add to what we have.

> It's a tiny little room, almost a closet, with walls that are dingy.

With is a great choice for a preposition to add additional information. Is there a shorter way we could say *walls that are dingy*? What about *floor that is concrete*?

> It's a tiny little room, almost a closet, with dingy walls and a concrete floor.

Tip Thatery and Whichery

Ken Macrorie (1988) considers the use of *that* a sin against a sentence. In these cases, *walls that are dingy* and *floor that is concrete* can be economized by shifting the adjective up front and close to what's being modified or described: dingy walls, a concrete floor. But *that* is not always a bad word. It's a word *that* can be useful, though we do agree with Macrorie in this case: *It's a useful word* is a more economical sentence.

The last three sentences talk about the lightbulb in the room.

> The room has one lightbulb.
> The lightbulb dangles from the ceiling.
> The lightbulb dangles in a way that's slightly creepy.

It looks like the lightbulb is part of a list, and before the third item in a list we can use a coordinating conjunction. Here *and* would work. How can we revise the other ideas for our revision? Talk it out with students.

> It's a tiny little room, almost a closet, with dingy walls, a concrete floor, and a lightbulb that dangles from the ceiling.

From the ceiling is a prepositional phrase, and we can add *in a slightly creepy way* to give detail about the way it dangles.

It's a tiny little room, almost a closet, with dingy walls, a concrete floor, and a lightbulb that dangles from the ceiling in a slightly creepy way.

Let's compare it to Stead's sentence to see the effects of our choices—and hers.

It's a tiny little room, almost a closet, with dingy walls, a concrete floor, and one lightbulb that dangles from the ceiling in a way that's slightly creepy.

Discuss the differences.

THE PRACTICE

Students grapple with the following cluster of sentences with a partner, using DRAFTing questions to revise in more than one way and then selecting their favorite (see Appendix G). They are now trying on the role of revisers. We look at another sentence based on *Liar & Spy*.

The only thing in the room is a table.
It's a folding table.
The table has metal legs.
The legs are spindly.

Students share revisions. Compare and contrast different responses, and then finally compare them with the original, reminding them that we look only to see other options.

The only thing in the room is a folding table with spindly metal legs.

Students evaluate similarities and differences between their own versions and the author's and the effects created by the different options. We reflect on their revision decisions by asking the following questions:

- What helped you most to revise the sentences?
- What are some patterns you noticed?
- Where would you use these patterns in your own writing? How would they help you as a writer?
- What questions do you still have?

THE COLLABORATION

We look at more sentences from Stead's book. Groups revise their assigned sentence in at least two ways and then select their favorite. In this case, read the first two sentences of the paragraph aloud before students revise the remaining clusters of complete sentences.

When I think of all the work Dad put into our house it's pretty sad. But mostly I feel sorry for myself, because the coolest thing about it was my room.

8.1 Dad took apart a fire escape a long time ago.
The fire escape was real.
The fire escape was from a building that his office was demolishing.
He rebuilt the bottom level of it.
He rebuilt it inside my bedroom.

8.2 He bolted it to a wall.
He attached a ladder to it.
The ladder was the original ladder.

8.3 I had a bed up there.
He made me cubbies.
These cubbies were built in.
The cubbies were for all of my stuff.

8.4 I had the most excellent room.
It was the best room of any kid I know.
We had to leave it behind.

Groups share their sentences in order, one at a time, displaying them so everyone can see them. As a class, consider them as a paragraph, making any revisions necessary for flow. Then compare the class paragraph to the original, not to correct but to consider the choices and the effects of those choices. What can we learn about our own writing from this comparison? What is our takeaway to write in our writer's notebook to remember for the future?

When I think of all the work Dad put into our house it's pretty sad. But mostly I feel sorry for myself, because the coolest thing about it was my room. A long time ago, Dad took apart a fire escape—a real fire escape, from a building that his office was demolishing—and he rebuilt the bottom level of it inside my bedroom. He bolted it to the wall, and even attached the original ladder. I had a bed up there, and he made me these built-in cubbies for all my stuff. I had the most excellent room of any kid I know, and we had to leave it behind.

THE APPLICATION

Looking for a Place

Students look through their writer's notebooks for a story seed. Writers consider the place (setting) of the story for a few moments, jotting down details they imagine in their mind's eye about the place. Then, students write a description of the place, using constructions similar to those studied in this lesson. Students share their writing with a partner and talk about what works in the description and what's missing.

In the Books

Students look through books or stories they've enjoyed reading for passages that set the scene. Tell them to consider the kind of language and structures authors use. They make a list of some good examples to bring to their writing groups, and then share the lists and note some patterns to share with the class.

Here are some examples from *The Tin Forest* by Helen Ward (2001), with prepositional phrases about location underlined:

> *Right <u>in the middle</u> was a small house, <u>with small windows</u>, that looked out <u>on other people's garbage and bad weather</u>.*
> *<u>In the house</u> lived an old man.*
> *He dreamed he lived <u>in a forest</u> full <u>of wild animals</u>.*
> *The old man spilled crumbs <u>from his sandwich</u> <u>onto the ground</u>.*
> *The bird ate the crumbs and perched to sing <u>in the branches</u> <u>of a tin tree</u>.*

Patterns:

1. Often the details in prepositional phrases come at the end of a sentence, after the main idea.
2. But sometimes the prepositional phrase is at the beginning of the sentence.
3. Lots of prepositional phrases answer the question "where?" and some answer "what kind?"

Titles FROM Prepositional Phrases

Students search through their writer's notebooks or writing folders for a piece they are currently working on. Writers generate titles for a few pieces of writing, using prepositions as starter words to create prepositional phrase titles. Here are some students' titles.

"In Trouble"
"After Eighth Grade"
"Before The Bell Rang"
"With Fries and a Coke"

Next time they are looking *for* a title, look *into* prepositional phrases. Discuss what other grammatical constructions we've learned about that could make good titles.

LESSON SET

9

THE *COMMA*-DRAMA DILEMMA
Use It . . . or Lose It?

Once students start revising, they get a little comma happy, attempting to add the common comma everywhere. It is, in fact, the most used punctuation mark. But although commas are quite helpful in corralling information this way or that, this lesson reminds us that we don't always need them— although in a few cases, we still really do.

In this lesson, we work against the grain and do something we rarely do. We show writers errors, so they can identify how using too many commas creates comma-tose writing.

Display the passages below and ask, "What's the difference, writers?"

I heard the story of the Pilgrims, many times from my grandparents and teachers, before I realized that the Pilgrims had shown up, in New England, without food or shelter six weeks, before winter.

I heard the story of the Pilgrims many times from my grandparents and teachers before I realized that the Pilgrims had shown up in New England without food or shelter six weeks before winter.

Students respond to reflective questions:

* Why do you think that?
* What is the effect created?

We notice that commas break up the first passage; we conclude that everything doesn't need to be separated by commas, and that commas can be real jerks . . . to our readers, literally jerking them out of the meaning. The second, correctly comma-less sentence is the one that made it into Charles C. Mann's *Before Columbus: The Americas of 1491* (2009).

THE POINTS OF EMPHASIS

- Commas
- Effects of punctuation
- Sentence variety
- Apostrophes
- Syntax
- Repetition

THE DEMONSTRATION

To demonstrate the effective use of commas, we read another excerpt from Mann's *Before Columbus* aloud twice. Students pay attention to how the author closes the chapter by summing up. He uses the organizational strategy of classification, grouping or categorizing advantages and disadvantages.

> *The lack of livestock was one of the major differences between the Indians and the Europeans who came to the Americas. Unlike the Europeans, the Indians did not live in constant contact with many animals. This had disadvantages—without horses, for example, Indians could not travel as fast or communicate as efficiently as Europeans.*
>
> *Life without livestock also had advantages. It let Indians escape many diseases. Scientists use the term* zoonotic disease *to mean an illness that can travel from animals to humans, and there are a lot of them. Influenza is one well-known zoonotic disease. It can start in birds and migrate to people, becoming an epidemic of "bird flu." A cattle disease becomes measles in humans. When a condition called horsepox jumps to humans, it is known as smallpox. The Americas were free from these and many more zoonotic diseases. That was a blessing for Indians who lived in isolation from the rest of the world. When the Europeans arrived, though, it became a deadly curse.*

Students share observations about the categories (or groupings of advantages and disadvantages) they notice.

Display the following cluster of sentences to revise as a class:

One major difference was a lack of livestock.
The difference was between the Indians and Europeans.
The Indians and Europeans who came to the Americas were different.

Students refer to the DRAFT mnemonic posted on the wall or on a handout (see Appendix G) to help us make our revision decisions. We begin by rearranging:

The lack of livestock was one major difference.

Now we delete the repeating three words of the second sentence: *the difference was*. And we can add *between the Indians and Europeans*. We talk this out.

> The lack of livestock was one major difference between the Indians and Europeans.

Yep, we don't need a comma to set off this prepositional phrase. We note that the third sentence sounds the same. Is there anything new here? Oh, our sentence doesn't refer to the Americas yet. We delete the repetition of *The Indians and Europeans* and add the information about the Americas to the end.

> The lack of livestock was one of the major differences between the Indians and the Europeans who came to the Americas.

And the "who clause"—the relative clause headed by the relative pronoun *who*—doesn't need a comma here either, because the clause's information is essential to the meaning of the sentence. We aren't talking about any Europeans, just those who came to the Americas.

THE PRACTICE

Student partners revise the three sentence clusters from Mann's *Before Columbus*:

Cluster 1

Scientists use the term *zoonotic disease*.
Zoonotic disease means an illness.
The illness can travel from animals to humans.
A lot of diseases travel from animals to humans.

Cluster 2

Influenza is one zoonotic disease.
Influenza is well known.

Cluster 3

It can start in birds.
Then it can migrate to people.
It can become an epidemic.
The epidemic can be "bird flu."

Writers use the DRAFT mnemonic to revise the sentences, combining for more than one variation. They star their favorite sentences and share their revisions, comparing and contrasting the different responses. Last, writers compare their versions with the author's original to acquire other options.

> *Scientists use the term* zoonotic disease *to mean an illness that can travel from animals to humans, and there are a lot of them. Influenza is one well-known zoonotic disease. It can start in birds and migrate to people, becoming an epidemic of "bird flu."*

Students evaluate similarities and differences between their own versions and the author's and the effects created by the different options. We reflect on their revision decisions by asking the following questions:

- What helped you most to revise the sentences?
- What are some patterns you noticed?
- Where would you use these patterns in your own writing? How would they help you as a writer?
- What questions do you have now?

THE COLLABORATION

Benjamin Bennaker is a famous inventor. We read to find out what he invented in our sentences from Andrea Pinkney's book *Hand in Hand: Ten Black Men Who Changed America* (2012). Groups revise their assigned sentences in at least two ways and then select their favorite. One of their choices is whether to use commas. Here they must face the comma-drama dilemma. Sometimes they're needed, sometimes not. This lesson gives us a chance to understand when commas are needed and when they're not. Groups think carefully about each comma they use—or lose.

After they have revised their sentences, have them write a quick explanation for each comma's use. Then ask these questions:

- Why did you choose to use it?
- What would be the effect if you did not?
- Does this use of a comma connect to any rule you know?

If groups choose not to use a comma, they should be prepared to explain that choice as well.

9.1 Things occurred to Benjamin.
His farm could function even more efficiently.
Putting things on a schedule would be efficient.
He could use the schedule of a clock.
He could schedule the day's waking, hauling, rinsing, rolling, and baking on this schedule.

9.2 Clocks weren't common.

Not everybody had one in the 1700s.

This was especially true for regular folks.

Folks such as farmers were regular folks.

But Benjamin's way of approaching the world was far from regular.

9.3 (Try starting with *Though*.)

He had never seen a timepiece.

He didn't know how a clock worked.

He set out to build one.

He would be using wood pieces.

The pieces were from Stout's timber shed.

9.4 He borrowed a watch.

The watch was a pocket watch.

He studied its innards.

He got to work.

9.5 The man was math-happy.

He drew plans for clocks.

He carved cogs.

He fashioned the clock's face.

He fashioned the hands of the clock.

He added a bell.

Groups share their sentences, displaying them so that everyone can see them. Discuss how the sentences flow together, and make adjustments as necessary. Compare the students' constructions with Pinkney's original text. How are they alike and how are they different? What are the effects of the differences?

> *It occurred to Benjamin that his farm could function even more efficiently by putting the day's waking, hauling, rinsing, rolling, and baking on a clock's schedule. Clocks weren't common in the 1700s, especially for regular folk such as farmers. But Benjamin's way of approaching the world was far from regular. Though he had never seen a timepiece and didn't know how a clock worked, he set out to build one using wood pieces from Stout's timber shed. He borrowed a pocket watch, studied its innards, and got to work. The math-happy man drew clock plans, carved cogs, fashioned the clock's face and hands, and added a bell.*

In this passage, commas serve mostly two purposes: separating items in a series and separating an introductory clause from the rest of the sentence.

One comma is used for a right-branching element. With a light touch, use this as a time to review or clarify grammatical understandings.

THE APPLICATION

Developing Comma-n Sense

Students look in their reading for sentences that use commas. They find sentences that look like they need a comma or don't. Students bring them to class and in small groups come up with explanations for why the authors made the choices they did. Students consider these questions:

* How did the use of commas help the authors communicate their message?
* Why might an author choose not to use a comma?

For example, in James Joyce's *Dubliners* (2012), why did he choose to forgo the comma in this lovely compound sentence? How would it change if it had a comma?"

The cold air stung us and we played till our bodies glowed.

Un-Comma-n Writing

Students look in their writer's notebooks for sentences they have written that use commas or that might use them. They highlight at least three of these sentences. Students then talk to a writing partner about their sentences and decide with that person if the use of commas (or lack of use) is the best choice for their purposes. They write in their notebooks their reasons for using or not using commas in those three sentences.

Inventing with Commas

In this lesson, we read about Benjamin Bennaker and one of his inventions. Another Benjamin was also an inventor as well as a founding father. Benjamin Franklin is known for inventing bifocals, lightning rods, the Franklin stove, the odometer, and swim fins; he also came up with the idea of daylight saving time and street lighting. Students write a sentence about Benjamin Franklin and his inventions, and then discuss, "Did you use a comma? Did you need to? Why?"

LESSON SET

WHAT'S LEFT?
Branching Out in New Ways

Sentences grow in a variety of ways. Most often they branch to the right, with added information or details following the **base clause**, or **main idea**, of the sentence, as in Sarah Albee's *Bugged* (2014, bold added): "**Bugs have affected the outcome of nearly every war ever fought**, because bugs carry diseases, including typhus, plague, cholera, yellow fever, malaria, typhoid, and dysentery."

In contrast, a left-branching sentence puts new material, details, and descriptions *ahead* of the base clause. The delay in getting to the **base clause** creates suspense. What if Sarah Albee had delayed the **base clause**? (*Because bugs carry diseases, including typhus, plague, cholera, yellow fever, malaria, typhoid, and dysentery,* **bugs have affected the outcome of nearly every war ever fought**.)

To consider the effects created by both right- and left-branching sentences, students compare Sarah Albee's original from *Bugged* (2014) to the left-branching alternative:

> *Bugs have affected the outcome of nearly every war ever fought, because bugs carry diseases, including typhus, plague, cholera, yellow fever, malaria, typhoid, and dysentery.*
>
> Because bugs carry diseases, including typhus, plague, cholera, yellow fever, malaria, typhoid, and dysentery, bugs have affected the outcome of nearly every war ever fought.

Students react to the effects created by the two structures. Ask follow-up questions to deepen the conversation:

- Why do you think that?
- How does the structure create that effect?

The second version is probably the most common kind of left-branching sentence, in which a subordinate clause or a series of clauses and phrases come before the **base clause**. By putting the clauses and phrases first, we see that the emphasis in the sentence is not on diseases but on their impact on history.

But left-branching (LB) can occur with a variety of structures. Here's a different example from *Guess What?* by Mem Fox (1998) where the subject and verb are delayed and inverted (the subject is toward the end of the sentence, with the verb before it). Students compare the different versions and discuss their effects.

> *Far away from here lives a crazy lady called Daisy O'Grady.*
>
> Daisy O'Grady, a crazy lady, lives far away from here.
>
> A crazy lady called Daisy O'Grady lives far away from here.

When students compare sentences with different structures, they see how their choices about arrangement affect tone and emphasis. Alternative sentence patterns give us—and all writers—a chance to consider what is important and what we want to emphasize through our syntactical choice.

Mid-branching sentences (a.k.a. interrupters) insert an aside in the middle of the sentence to delay the conclusion of a thought as a way to create suspense. In this lesson, we are looking at sentences that branch in specific places—between subject and verb or between a verb and its object. Students compare this set of sentences, one the original from and one derived from Heather Lynn Miller's *This Is Your Life Cycle* (2008), and discuss their effects:

> *Then one day, your egg casing split, and* **you***—a white wiggling nymph—***slipped** *into the open water of the pond.*
>
> You are a white wiggling nymph and one day your egg casing split and you slipped into the open water of the pond.

Challenges of Left-Branching and Mid-Branching Sentences

For writers, the challenge of using left-branching or mid-branching sentences is the possibility of losing track of the sentence's point. Sometimes left branches or mid-branches (interrupters) get so long that the base clause is forgotten. Or sometimes the information in the left branch isn't appropriate for the opening of the sentence. Virginia Tufte (2006) finds that the best uses of left- branching sentences are when "there is a temporal or logical development that invites the delayed disclosure" inherent in this structure (174). Readers can get lost if writers don't draw a clear path through the clauses and phrases that introduce or interrupt the main part—or base clause—of the sentence.

THE POINTS OF EMPHASIS

- Prepositional phrases
- Participial phrases
- Commas after introductory elements and in a series
- Appositives
- Subordinate clauses

THE DEMONSTRATION

To demonstrate the way sentences can branch in the middle or to the left, display the following cluster of sentences derived from Gail Gibbons's *Pirates: Robbers of the High Seas* (1993):

> Something happened around 1300.
> Pirates set up settlements.
> The pirates were in bands.
> The pirates were ruthless.
> The settlements were along the coast.
> The coast was in North Africa.

Reading the whole cluster of sentences helps us get an idea of the sentence we could be creating. It allows us to sort a lot of information and gives us possibilities for structuring our ideas into a sentence others will understand. Which elements of our DRAFTing strategies can help us start that revising? With the first two ideas, if we keep them in order, we get something like this:

> Around 1300, pirates set up settlements.

That looks like what we are used to, right? Now what do we do with the next few sentences that describe the pirates? If we do what we usually do in English, those describing words—adjectives—come before the noun.

> Around 1300, bands of ruthless pirates set up settlements.

Good. Now the revision with the next one seems logical. It's about the settlements and where they were, so we can add to the right—the most common kind of adding (or branching).

> Around 1300, bands of ruthless pirates set up settlements along the coast.

We could delete some words by changing our prepositional phrase into a modifier. Then our sentence would be more economical.

> Around 1300, bands of ruthless pirates set up coastal settlements.

That would keep the meaning of the sentence. It's good to think about different ways of seeing the revisions. But if we choose to eliminate that prepositional phrase, how do we add the next sentence's information? We could say this, perhaps:

> Around 1300, bands of ruthless pirates set up North African coastal settlements.

However, we might want to return to the original and keep the prepositional phrase:

> Around 1300, bands of ruthless pirates set up settlements along the North African coast.

Or even keep two prepositional phrases:

> Around 1300, bands of ruthless pirates set up settlements along the coast of North Africa.

We ask students, "What is the difference? Which do you like better? Why?"

Before we leave this sentence and go to our groups for revising, we look once more at what we have and compare it with Gail Gibbon's original (bold added).

> *Around 1300, **bands of ruthless** pirates set up settlements along the North African coast.*

"We (and Gibbons) have several words before we get to the actual subject of this sentence, don't we?" we say. "Sometimes we will have adjectives with our subject, but in this sentence we have more than that: a left-branching sentence. We are familiar with right-branching sentences, where the main idea comes at the beginning of the sentence and then details are added after. Left-branching sentences grow on the left side, with details *before* the base clause. What effect do you think the author wanted to create by beginning this sentence with more information? Why didn't she write *around 1300* at the end of the sentence? It could work there, so why do you think she chose to put it at the beginning?"

Tip Commas with Introductory Elements

The general rule of thumb is that writers don't need commas with short introductory elements of four or fewer words. However, often the comma is needed for clarity, as in this example: *Around 1300, pirates pillaged* vs. *Around 1300 pirates pillaged.*

THE PRACTICE

Students tussle with the following simple sentences with a partner, trying on the role of revisers, revising for more than one construction and starring the one they like best. They continue using the DRAFT strategies as needed (see Appendix G).

> Something happened for many years.
> They attacked ships.
> They looted ships.
> The ships sailed off the coast.
> The coast was by their settlement.
> The settlement was called the Barbary States.

Students share revisions. The class compares and contrasts different responses, and then finally they compare their revisions with Gail Gibbons's original, remembering that we're looking to see other options.

> *For many years they attacked and looted ships that sailed off the coast*
> *of their settlement, the Barbary States.*

Writers evaluate similarities and differences between their own versions and the author's and the effects created by the different options. We reflect on their revision decisions by asking the following questions:

- What helped you most to revise the sentences?
- What are some patterns you noticed?
- Where would you use these patterns in your own writing? How would they help you as a writer?
- What did we learn about left-branching sentences? Why might a writer choose that construction?
- What questions do you still have?

THE COLLABORATION

Groups revise their assigned sentence in at least two ways and then select their favorite.

10.1 These people were known.
     They were known as the Barbary pirates.
     The Barbary pirates were famous.

10.2 Something happened five hundred years ago.
     Spain discovered fine goods and treasures.
     The fine goods and treasures were of the New World.
     Pirates became a danger.
     They became a special danger.

10.3 The news spread among the pirates.

The news was of Spanish treasure ships.

The ships were carrying emeralds.

The ships were carrying gold.

The ships were carrying silver.

The ships were carrying pearls.

The ships were carrying other cargo.

The ships were carrying these treasures back to Europe.

10.4 The Spanish traders sailed ships.

The ships were large.

The ships were armed.

The ships were called galleons.

10.5 The pirates watched for the galleons.

They watched for returning galleons.

They especially watched for ships coming from major trading ports.

The major trading ports were Havana, Cartagena, and Porto Bello.

Groups share their sentences, displaying them so everyone can see them. The class puts the sentences in a paragraph, revising to improve flow as necessary. Compare the class construction to the original text, with the goal of being able to discuss the effects of the choices, not to correct. How are they alike and how are they different? What are the different effects created by the different choices writers made?

> *Around 1300, bands of ruthless pirates set up settlements along the North African coast. For many years they attacked and looted ships that sailed off the coast of their settlement, the Barbary States. These people were known as the famous Barbary pirates. About five hundred years ago, when Spain discovered the fine goods and treasures of the New World, pirates became a special danger. The news of Spanish treasure ships carrying emeralds, gold, silver, pearls, and other cargo back to Europe spread among the pirates. The Spanish traders sailed large armed ships called galleons. The pirates watched for the returning galleons, especially those coming from the major trading ports of Havana, Cartagena, and Porto Bello.*

THE APPLICATION

Pirating Others' Sentences

Students collect one or two left-branching and mid-branching sentences from a book they are reading or from texts in the classroom to share with a group. An example of a left-branching sentence is this one (bold added) from Loreen Leedy's *Tracks in the Sand* (1993):

During the quiet night, while the air is cool, the turtles escape from their chambers.

Two examples of mid-branching sentences where the interruption comes between the verb and its object are these from Robert Burleigh's picture-book biography of artist Georges Seurat, *Seurat and La Grande Jatte* (2004). In these sentences (bold added), Burleigh is describing the post-impressionist style Seurat created, pointillism:

The French word point *means—**that's right**—point or dot.*
*He was—**as a friend put it**—"haunted by night's magnificence."*

Remind students that right-, left-, or mid-branches can be set off with commas or dashes.

In groups of three, students compile examples and place them in categories. They should name the categories and be ready to share some of their observations.

Pirating Your Own Sentences

Students find two or three sentences in their writer's notebook that are either right-branching or that have only a base clause. Students will rewrite each one as a left-branching and mid-branching sentence. Here's an example I pulled from my writer's notebook and my rewritings of it:

I found the candy in the dirt on the side of the road.

Left: On the side of the road, in the dirt, *I found the candy.*
Mid-: I found—*in the dirt on the side of the road*—the candy.

Then students work with a partner to talk out the effect of each sentence structure. Tell them, "If you like the pirated sentence better, use it; if it isn't doing the work you need, explain why in the margin next to the sentence in your notebook." (By the way, I decided I liked the LB sentence best. This is the first sentence in a memoir essay, and waiting to put what I found at the end creates the suspense I want for the first sentence of my piece.)

Pillaging Your Paper

Students select a piece of their own writing. Each student rereads the selected piece, identifying right-branching, left-branching, and mid-branching sentences they have used. Writers use a reviser's shorthand to identify branch types (RB, LB, MB). If they don't have any, they scour for spots to add one or two. Then they share the results with a writing partner, talking about the choices they made and why they made them.

APPENDIXES

(The appendix pages may be printed from www.stenhouse.com/revision-decisions.)

Appendixes A through E support the sample lesson described in Chapter 3.

Appendixes F and G are charts referred to in various lesson sets.

APPENDIX Chapter 3: The Context

Flames shot up, igniting the line of hanging paper patterns.

Flames shot up into the air.

The flames ignited paper patterns that were hanging.

The patterns were on a line that hung across the room.

Excerpt from Albert Marrin's *Flesh and Blood So Cheap* (2011).

APPENDIX   **B**   Chapter 3: The Demonstration

The invention of the sprinkler created possibilities.

It was possible to drown a fire.

It would take only seconds.

Revision Decisions: Talking Through Sentences and Beyond by Jeff Anderson and Deborah Dean. Copyright © 2014. Stenhouse Publishers.

APPENDIX Chapter 3: The Practice

Heat rose from the fire.

The heat triggered the fuses.

The fuses automatically released a deluge of water.

The water had been stored in overhead sprinkler pipes.

Revision Decisions: Talking Through Sentences and Beyond by Jeff Anderson and Deborah Dean. Copyright © 2014. Stenhouse Publishers.

 Chapter 3: The Collaboration

Cluster 1
It took minutes.
146 workers died.
They ended up broken on the sidewalk.
Others were suffocated by smoke.
Many were burnt in the flames.

Cluster 2
Most were young women.
They were ages fourteen to twenty-three.
Nearly all were recent immigrants.
They were mostly Italians and Russian
    Jews.

Cluster 3
It was dubbed the "Triangle Fire."
It held the record for New York's
    deadliest workplace fire.
It held the record for ninety years.

Cluster 4
Only the September 11, 2001, terrorist
    attacks took more lives.
Those attacks were on the World Trade
    Center.

Revision Decisions: Talking Through Sentences and Beyond by Jeff Anderson and Deborah Dean. Copyright © 2014. Stenhouse Publishers.

APPENDIX Chapter 3: Excerpt from *Flesh and Blood So Cheap* by Albert Marrin (2011).

Within minutes, 146 workers died, broken on the sidewalk, suffocated by smoke, or burnt in the flames. Most were young women ages fourteen to twenty-three, nearly all recent immigrants, Italians and Russian Jews. Dubbed the "Triangle Fire," for ninety years it held the record as New York's deadliest workplace fire. Only the September 11, 2001, terrorist attacks on the World Trade Center took more lives.

Revision Decisions: Talking Through Sentences and Beyond by Jeff Anderson and Deborah Dean. Copyright © 2014. Stenhouse Publishers.

APPENDIX Charting Connections

Prepositions

What do they do? *Show time and place as well as introduce examples, contrasts, or comparisons.*

Function	Example
Time	*at, in, on*
Extended Time	*since, for, by, from, to, until, during, with(in)*
Direction	*to, toward, on, onto, in, into*
Location	*above, across, against, ahead of, along, among, around, at, by, behind, below, beside, beneath, between, from, in, inside, on, off, out of, over, near, through, toward, under, within*
Introduce Examples and Comparisons or Contrasts	*as, despite, except, for, like, of, per, than, with, without*

Relative Pronouns

What do they do? *Introduce and link additional information to the noun before it.*

Function	Example
Link **ideas and things** to more detail	*that, what, which*
Link **people** to more detail	*who, whoever, whose, whom*

Connector Punctuation

What do they do? *Combine, introduce, and enclose information.*

Combines	Introduces	Encloses
Comma **,**		Comma **,**
Dash —	Dash —	Dash —
Semicolon **;**	Colon **:**	Parentheses **( )**
		Quotation Marks **" "**

Subordinating Conjunctions (AAWWUBBIS)

Although
After
While
When
Until
Because
Before
If
Since

What do they do? *Show relationships, sometimes making one idea more or less important.*

Function	Example
Time	*after, before, during, since, until, when, whenever, while*
Cause-Effect	*as, because, since, so*
Opposition	*although, even though, though, while, whatever*
Condition	*as long as, if, in order to, unless, until, whatever*

Coordinating Conjunctions (FANBOYS)

For
And
Nor
But
Or
Yet
So

What do they do? *Make connections that are equal to each other. They join sentences (compound) and they can also show a relationship between a pair or a list.*

Function	Example
Combine	*and*
Opposition	*but, yet, nor*
Cause-Effect	*so, for*
Choice	*or*

APPENDIX Decisions Writers Make

Revision Decisions		
DRAFT	**Revision**	**Decision**
D	**Delete** unnecessary and repeated words	Is there any needless repetition or words that don't add anything?
R	**Rearrange** words, phrases, or clauses	Should anything be moved around or rearranged?
A	**Add** connectors	Can I communicate more directly or economically if I add a new word(s) or punctuation to show relationships?
F	**Form** new verb endings	Could I change the form of any verbs to make my sentence smoother and more compact?
T	**Talk** it out	How do various versions and changes sound when I talk them out? Does it sound right? Is it smooth?

Revision Decisions: Talking Through Sentences and Beyond by Jeff Anderson and Deborah Dean. Copyright © 2014. Stenhouse Publishers.

APPENDIXES

for Lesson Sets

1 Through 10

(The appendix pages may be printed from www.stenhouse.com/revision-decisions.)

Appendixes 1.1 through 10.4 provide four print or display resources (context, practice, collaboration, and the relevant literature excerpt) for each of the ten lesson sets.

APPENDIX | **1.1** | Lesson Set 1: The Context

Honeybees create hives, **labyrinths of wax honeycomb in which they store honey and raise their young**.

A rat can collapse its skeleton, **allowing it to wriggle through a hole as narrow as three-quarters of an inch**.

Bees, wasps, and ants belong to an order of insects called Hymenoptera, **which means "membranous wings."**

Excerpts from Jim Arnosky's *Creep and Flutter: The Secret World of Insects and Spiders* (2012) and from Albert Marrin's *Oh, Rats! The Story of Rats and People* (2006).

Revision Decisions: Talking Through Sentences and Beyond by Jeff Anderson and Deborah Dean. Copyright © 2014. Stenhouse Publishers.

APPENDIX 1.2 Lesson Set 1: The Practice

He looked around the café.

It was deserted.

The 7UP clock ticked.

It was loud and lonely.

It was on the far wall.

Revision Decisions: Talking Through Sentences and Beyond by Jeff Anderson and Deborah Dean. Copyright © 2014. Stenhouse Publishers.

APPENDIX 1.3   Lesson Set 1: The Collaboration

1.1   It was before dawn and still dark.
It was August 26, 1929.
A boy was in the back of a small house.
It was in Torrance, California.
The boy was twelve years old.
He sat up in bed.
He listened.

1.2   There was a sound.
It was coming from outside.
The sound was growing.
It grew ever louder.

1.3   It was huge.
It was a rush.
The rush was heavy.
It suggested immensity.
It suggested a great parting of air.

1.4   It was coming from directly above the house.
The boy swung his legs.
He swung them off his bed.
He raced down the stairs.
He slapped open the back door.
He loped onto the grass.

1.5   The yard was otherworldly.
The yard was smothered in darkness.
The darkness was unnatural.
The yard was shivering with sound.

1.6   The boy stood on the lawn.
He was beside his brother.
His brother was older.
His head was thrown back.
He was spellbound.

Revision Decisions: Talking Through Sentences and Beyond by Jeff Anderson and Deborah Dean. Copyright © 2014. Stenhouse Publishers.

APPENDIX Lesson Set 1: Excerpt from Laura Hillenbrand's *Unbroken: A World War II Story of Survival, Resilience, and Redemption* (2010).

In the predawn darkness of August 26, 1929, in the back of a small house in Torrance, California, a twelve-year-old boy sat up in bed, listening. There was a sound coming from outside, growing ever louder. It was a huge, heavy rush, suggesting immensity, a great parting of air. It was coming from directly above the house. The boy swung his legs off his bed, raced down the stairs, slapped open the back door, and loped onto the grass. The yard was otherworldly, smothered in unnatural darkness, shivering with sound. The boy stood on the lawn beside his older brother, head thrown back, spellbound.

Revision Decisions: Talking Through Sentences and Beyond by Jeff Anderson and Deborah Dean. Copyright © 2014. Stenhouse Publishers.

APPENDIX **2.1**   Lesson Set 2: The Context

Many people overlook the benefits that insects bring. Useful products are derived from insects. Honey and silk are derived from insects. Waxes are too. Oils are also derived from insects. In addition, natural medicines are derived from insects. Dyes are made from insects too.

Many people overlook the benefits that insects bring. Useful products derived from insects range from honey and silk to waxes, oils, natural medicines, and dyes.

Excerpt from George C. McGavin's *Smithsonian Handbooks: Insects* (2002).

Revision Decisions: Talking Through Sentences and Beyond by Jeff Anderson and Deborah Dean. Copyright © 2014. Stenhouse Publishers.

APPENDIX 2.2 Lesson Set 2: The Practice

Beetles are found in many shapes.

Beetles are found in many sizes.

Beetles are also found in many colors.

There is an amazing range of shapes, sizes, and colors.

Beetles all share the same basic design.

Revision Decisions: Talking Through Sentences and Beyond by Jeff Anderson and Deborah Dean. Copyright © 2014. Stenhouse Publishers.

APPENDIX 2.3   Lesson Set 2: The Collaboration

2.1   The lizard menu stretches.
       The menu stretches longer than a roll of toilet paper.
       The roll of toilet paper is unraveled.

2.2   They dine on a variety of dishes.
       The variety of dishes is wide.
       The variety includes plant dishes and animal dishes.

2.3   Other lizards are vegetarian.
       Vegetarians eat vegetation.
       The vegetation they eat is mainly leaves.
       The vegetation they eat is mainly flowers.
       The vegetation they eat is mainly fruit.

2.4   However, it is a fact that is true that most other lizard
           species have a diet.
       The diet is something they stick to.
       The diet is lively.

2.5   Anoles are an example or instance.
       Anoles provide pest-control services.
       Their pest control services are top-notch.
       They devour insects.

2.6   Other lizards eat almost anything that runs, crawls,
           flies, or breathes.
       They eat birds.
       They eat rodents.
       They eat worms.
       They eat deer.
       They eat other reptiles.

Revision Decisions: Talking Through Sentences and Beyond by Jeff Anderson and Deborah Dean. Copyright © 2014. Stenhouse Publishers.

APPENDIX Lesson Set 2: Excerpt from Sneed B. Collard III's *Most Fun Book Ever About Lizards* (2012).

The lizard menu stretches longer than an unraveled roll of toilet paper. Some lizards, such as the bearded dragon, are omnivores. They dine on a wide variety of plant and animal dishes. Other lizards, such as the common iguana, are vegetarian and eat mainly leaves, flowers, and fruit. However, most other lizard species stick to a lively diet. Anoles, for instance, provide top-notch pest-control services by devouring insects. Other lizards eat birds, rodents, worms, deer, other reptiles—almost anything that runs, crawls, flies, or breathes.

Revision Decisions: Talking Through Sentences and Beyond by Jeff Anderson and Deborah Dean. Copyright © 2014. Stenhouse Publishers.

APPENDIX **3.1** Lesson Set 3: The Context

It is important to understand that there are not two worlds: the world of humans and a separate world of plants and animals. There isn't a "natural world" and a "man-made world." We all live on the same planet and live in the same natural order.

Excerpt from Mark Kurlansky's *World Without Fish* (2011).

Revision Decisions: Talking Through Sentences and Beyond by Jeff Anderson and Deborah Dean. Copyright © 2014. Stenhouse Publishers.

APPENDIX **3.2** Lesson Set 3: The Practice

Electric wires were torn free.

They were broken.

They sizzled.

They sparked.

They were on the ground.

Revision Decisions: Talking Through Sentences and Beyond by Jeff Anderson and Deborah Dean. Copyright © 2014. Stenhouse Publishers.

APPENDIX | **3.3** | Lesson Set 3: The Collaboration

3.1   Train cars toppled.
        They toppled off the rails.
        Wagons overturned.
        The horses that had pulled them lay dead.
        They were still in their harnesses.

3.2   The wave cracked things.
        It cracked the hulls of ships.

3.3   It smashed things.
        It smashed decks.
        The smashing came from flying debris.

3.4   Some things happened in Dartmouth.
        The rope factory was little more than a pile.
        The beer brewery was little more than a pile.
        The piles were of brick.

3.5   Some things happened throughout both cities.
        Windows were shattered.
        The windows were in homes.
        The windows were in stores.
        The windows were in offices.
        The windows were in schools.
        All of the shattered windows made a blizzard.
        The blizzard was of glass.
        The blizzard was deadly.

Revision Decisions: Talking Through Sentences and Beyond by Jeff Anderson and Deborah Dean. Copyright © 2014. Stenhouse Publishers.

APPENDIX 3.4 Lesson Set 3: Excerpt from Sally Walker's *Blizzard of Glass: The Halifax Explosion of 1917* (2011).

The shock wave snapped telegraph poles and trees in two as easily as if they'd been twigs. Electric wires, torn free and broken, sizzled and sparked on the ground. Train cars toppled off the rails, wagons overturned, and the horses that had pulled them lay dead in their harnesses. The wave cracked the hulls of ships and smashed the decks with flying debris. In Dartmouth, the rope factory and beer brewery were little more than piles of brick. Throughout both cities, the windows in homes and stores and offices and schools shattered in a deadly blizzard of glass.

Revision Decisions: Talking Through Sentences and Beyond by Jeff Anderson and Deborah Dean. Copyright © 2014. Stenhouse Publishers.

APPENDIX 4.1   Lesson Set 4: The Context

Human hair mites get all they need from their hosts—us. They are tiny relatives of spiders, about one-tenth of a millimeter long (smaller than a grain of salt), with bodies like miniature salamis and four pairs of stumpy legs. They live in the roots of hair (usually eyelashes or eyebrows), where they munch on dead skin and sebum (the oily stuff that keeps hair shiny). The only time they wander is when young mites search for a hair of their own, when they may find their way onto another body.

Excerpt from Nicola Davies's *What's Eating You?* (2009).

Revision Decisions: Talking Through Sentences and Beyond by Jeff Anderson and Deborah Dean. Copyright © 2014. Stenhouse Publishers.

APPENDIX **4.2** Lesson Set 4: The Practice

Dry pet foods caught on during World War II.

The dry pet foods were cereal-based.

Tin-rationing put a stop to canning.

Tin-rationing included the canning of dog food.

The dog food was made from horse meat.

There was an abundance around the time Americans embraced the automobile.

They began selling their mounts to the knackers.

Revision Decisions: Talking Through Sentences and Beyond by Jeff Anderson and Deborah Dean. Copyright © 2014. Stenhouse Publishers.

APPENDIX 4.3 Lesson Set 4: The Collaboration

4.1   Rodents are not like cats.
       Rodents are controlled by sweetness.
       Cats are not controlled by sweetness.
       One could say that rodents are slaves to sweetness.

4.2   Rats have been known to die.
       They die from not getting enough nutrition.
       A lack of nutrition is called malnutrition.
       Rather than step away from a drip of sugar water,
           rats die of malnutrition.

4.3   This was shown in a study.
       The study was about obesity.
       The study was from the 1970s.
       Rats were fed a supermarket diet.
       The diet was all you can eat.
       The diet included marshmallows.
       It also included milk chocolate and chocolate-chip
           cookies.
       The rats gained 269 percent more weight than rats
           fed standard laboratory fare.

4.4   There are strains of mice.
       Some strains will consume their own body weight.
       They will consume their body weight in diet soda.
       They will do this over the course of a day.
       You do not want the job of changing their bedding.

Revision Decisions: Talking Through Sentences and Beyond by Jeff Anderson and Deborah Dean. Copyright © 2014. Stenhouse Publishers.

APPENDIX Lesson Set 4: Excerpt from Mary Roach's *Gulp: Adventures on the Alimentary Canal* (2013).

Rodents, on the other hand, are slaves to sweetness. They have been known to die of malnutrition rather than step away from a sugar-water drip. In an obesity study from the 1970s, rats fed an all-you-can-eat "supermarket" diet that included marshmallows, milk chocolate, and chocolate-chip cookies gained 269 percent more weight than rats fed standard laboratory fare. There are strains of mice that will, over the course of a day, consume their own body weight in diet soda, and you do not want the job of changing their bedding.

Revision Decisions: Talking Through Sentences and Beyond by Jeff Anderson and Deborah Dean. Copyright © 2014. Stenhouse Publishers.

APPENDIX **5.1** Lesson Set 5: The Context

Fats Domino was another singer.

He sang rock and roll.

He put the sound of New Orleans in his music.

Fats Domino, another early rock & roll singer, put the sound of New Orleans in his music.

Excerpt from Holly George-Warren's *Shake, Rattle & Roll: The Founders of Rock and Roll* (2001).

Revision Decisions: Talking Through Sentences and Beyond by Jeff Anderson and Deborah Dean. Copyright © 2014. Stenhouse Publishers.

APPENDIX 5.2   Lesson Set 5: The Practice

One day something happened.

It happened when Albert was sick.

He was sick in bed.

The happening was that his father brought him something.

It was a compass.

A compass was a small case.

It was a round case.

Inside was a magnetic needle.

Revision Decisions: Talking Through Sentences and Beyond by Jeff Anderson and Deborah Dean. Copyright © 2014. Stenhouse Publishers.

APPENDIX **5.3**   Lesson Set 5: The Collaboration

5.1   Something didn't matter.
It didn't matter which way Albert turned the compass.
The needle always pointed north.
It was as if it were held.
The holding was by an invisible hand.

5.2   Albert was so amazed.
His amazement made his body tremble.

5.3   Suddenly he knew something.
He knew there were mysteries.
The mysteries were in the world.
The mysteries were hidden.
The mysteries were silent.
The mysteries were unknown.
The mysteries were unseen.

5.4   He wanted something.
He wanted it more than anything.
He wanted to understand those mysteries.

Revision Decisions: Talking Through Sentences and Beyond by Jeff Anderson and Deborah Dean. Copyright © 2014. Stenhouse Publishers.

APPENDIX Lesson Set 5: Excerpt from Jennifer Berne's *On a Beam of Light: A Story of Albert Einstein* (2013).

One day, when Albert was sick in bed, his father brought him a compass—a small round case with a magnetic needle inside. No matter which way Albert turned the compass, the needle always pointed north, as if held by an invisible hand. Albert was so amazed his body trembled. Suddenly he knew there were mysteries in the world—hidden and silent, unknown and unseen. He wanted, more than anything, to understand those mysteries.

Revision Decisions: Talking Through Sentences and Beyond by Jeff Anderson and Deborah Dean. Copyright © 2014. Stenhouse Publishers.

APPENDIX 6.1 Lesson Set 6: The Context

The man stood very still.

The man was looking at us.

The man tried to focus his eyes in the sudden light.

The man stood there very still, looking at us, trying to focus his eyes in the sudden light.

Excerpt from Adina Rishe Gerwitz's *Zebra Forest* (2013).

Revision Decisions: Talking Through Sentences and Beyond by Jeff Anderson and Deborah Dean. Copyright © 2014. Stenhouse Publishers.

APPENDIX **6.2** Lesson Set 6: The Practice

The front feet are wide.

They show in bear tracks.

They show completely.

The hind feet are large.

They show in bear tracks.

They show completely.

Revision Decisions: Talking Through Sentences and Beyond by Jeff Anderson and Deborah Dean. Copyright © 2014. Stenhouse Publishers.

APPENDIX 6.3 Lesson Set 6: The Collaboration

6.1   The front feet show up.
        They show up in the tracks.
        The front portion of the hind feet show up.
        They show up in the tracks.
        They show up when the bear is running.

6.2   A bear is a heavy animal.
        The heaviness makes something happen.
        Its tracks are pressed.
        They are pressed deeply.
        They are pressed often.
        They create defined footprints.
        The definition is perfect.

6.3   An experienced tracker can estimate.
        A tracker uses a set of footprints.
        A perfect set of footprints is two front and two hind.
        A tracker can estimate the size of the bear.
        The size is the size of the one that made the tracks.
        A tracker can estimate the weight of the bear.

6.4   A bear's toes spread apart.
        They do this on slippery surfaces.
        They do it for better traction.
        The spreading presses footprints.
        The footprints are large.
        They are larger than the bear's actual feet.

Revision Decisions: Talking Through Sentences and Beyond by Jeff Anderson and Deborah Dean. Copyright © 2014. Stenhouse Publishers.

APPENDIX 6.4 Lesson Set 6: Excerpt from Jim Arnosky's *Wild Tracks!* (2008)

Bears walk flat footed, placing the entire foot on the ground with each step. The wide front feet and the large hind feet show completely in bear tracks. When running, the front feet and the front portion of the hind feet show up in the tracks. Because a bear is a heavy animal, its tracks are often pressed deeply, creating perfectly defined footprints. With a perfect set of four bear footprints (two front and two hind), an experienced animal tracker is able to accurately estimate the size and weight of the bear that made them. On slippery surfaces, a bear's toes spread apart for better traction, pressing in footprints that are much larger than the bear's feet. Such splayed footprints can fool a tracker into imagining the bear that left them is much larger than its actual size.

Revision Decisions: Talking Through Sentences and Beyond by Jeff Anderson and Deborah Dean. Copyright © 2014. Stenhouse Publishers.

APPENDIX **7.1**   Lesson Set 7: The Context

Scientists in the late 1930s engaged in a frantic race. They were breaking atoms and working in secret facilities because they were trying to gain world dominance.

Scientists in the late 1930s engaged in a frantic race, breaking atoms, working in secret facilities, trying to gain world dominance.

Excerpt from Steve Sheinkin's *Bomb: The Race to Build—and Steal—the World's Most Dangerous Weapon* (2012).

Revision Decisions: Talking Through Sentences and Beyond by Jeff Anderson and Deborah Dean. Copyright © 2014. Stenhouse Publishers.

APPENDIX 7.2 Lesson Set 7: The Practice

He made notes.

He did this as he watched.

He watched the birds.

He wrote.

He wrote what the birds did.

He wrote how they behaved.

Revision Decisions: Talking Through Sentences and Beyond by Jeff Anderson and Deborah Dean. Copyright © 2014. Stenhouse Publishers.

APPENDIX 7.3   Lesson Set 7: The Collaboration

7.1   And he was like many.
      He was like young boys.
      He was a collector.

7.2   He collected things.
      He collected shells.
      He collected seals.
      He collected coins.
      He collected minerals.

7.3   He studied what he collected.
      He organized them by kind.
      His organization was in a tradition.
      The tradition was of natural historians.

7.4   His great love was hunting.
      Another great love was shooting.
      These loves came as he got older.

7.5   He shuddered.
      He shuddered later in life.
      He shuddered at something.
      The something was how many animals he had killed.

7.6   He quivered.
      He quivered with joy.
      He quivered with excitement.
      His quivering was before picking up a gun.
      His quivering was at the time of his youth.

Revision Decisions: Talking Through Sentences and Beyond by Jeff Anderson and Deborah Dean. Copyright © 2014. Stenhouse Publishers.

APPENDIX Lesson Set 7: Excerpt from Deborah Heiligman's *Charles and Emma: The Darwins' Leap of Faith* (2009).

Charles could entertain himself for hours just by thinking, or by observing birds, or watching sticks and leave float down a stream. <u>He</u> made notes as he watched the birds, writing down what they did, how they behaved. And like many young boys, he was a collector. <u>He</u> collected shells, seals, coins, and minerals. <u>He</u> studied them and organized them by kind—in the tradition of natural historians. <u>As he got older</u>, his great love was hunting and shooting. <u>Later in life</u> he shuddered at how many animals he had killed. But <u>at the time</u> he quivered with joy and excitement before picking up a gun.

Revision Decisions: Talking Through Sentences and Beyond by Jeff Anderson and Deborah Dean. Copyright © 2014. Stenhouse Publishers.

APPENDIX 8.1   Lesson Set 8: The Context

I just stood there, clutching the basketball tightly. A wild October wind whipped, rattling the windows.

I just stood there on the free-throw line, in the shadow of that big orange sign above the scoreboard, clutching the basketball tight to my chest. Outside, a wild October wind whipped through town, rattling the windows high above the bleachers in the gym.

Excerpt from L.D. Harkrader'a *Airball: My Life in Briefs* (2008).

Revision Decisions: Talking Through Sentences and Beyond by Jeff Anderson and Deborah Dean. Copyright © 2014. Stenhouse Publishers.

APPENDIX 8.2 Lesson Set 8: The Practice

The only thing in the room is a table.

It's a folding table.

The table has metal legs.

The legs are spindly.

Revision Decisions: Talking Through Sentences and Beyond by Jeff Anderson and Deborah Dean. Copyright © 2014. Stenhouse Publishers.

APPENDIX **8.3** Lesson Set 8: The Collaboration

When I think of all the work Dad put into our house it's pretty sad. But mostly I feel sorry for myself, because the coolest thing about it was my room.

8.1   Dad took apart a fire escape a long time ago.
        The fire escape was real.
        The fire escape was from a building that his
            office was demolishing.
        He rebuilt the bottom level of it.
        He rebuilt it inside my bedroom.

8.2   He bolted it to a wall.
        He attached a ladder to it.
        The ladder was the original ladder.

8.3   I had a bed up there.
        He made me cubbies.
        These cubbies were built in.
        The cubbies were for all of my stuff.

8.4   I had the most excellent room.
        It was the best room of any kid I know.
        We had to leave it behind.

Excerpt based on Rebecca Stead's *Liar & Spy* (2013)

APPENDIX Lesson Set 8: Excerpt from Rebecca Stead's *Liar & Spy* (2013).

When I think of all the work Dad put into our house it's pretty sad. But mostly I feel sorry for myself, because the coolest thing about it was my room. A long time ago, Dad took apart a fire escape—a real fire escape, from a building that his office was demolishing—and he rebuilt the bottom level of it inside my bedroom. He bolted it to the wall, and even attached the original ladder. I had a bed up there, and he made me these built-in cubbies for all my stuff. I had the most excellent room of any kid I know, and we had to leave it behind.

Revision Decisions: Talking Through Sentences and Beyond by Jeff Anderson and Deborah Dean. Copyright © 2014. Stenhouse Publishers.

APPENDIX 9.1   Lesson Set 9: The Context

I heard the story of the Pilgrims, many times from my grandparents and teachers, before I realized that the Pilgrims had shown up, in New England, without food or shelter six weeks, before winter.

I heard the story of the Pilgrims many times from my grandparents and teachers before I realized that the Pilgrims had shown up in New England without food or shelter six weeks before winter.

Excerpt from Charles C. Mann's *Before Columbus: The Americas of 1491* (2009).

Revision Decisions: Talking Through Sentences and Beyond by Jeff Anderson and Deborah Dean. Copyright © 2014. Stenhouse Publishers.

APPENDIX **9.2** Lesson Set 9: The Practice

Cluster 1
Scientists use the term *zoonotic disease*.
Zoonotic disease means an illness.
The illness can travel from animals to
    humans.
A lot of diseases travel from animals to
    humans.

Cluster 2
Influenza is one zoonotic disease.
Influenza is well known.

Cluster 3
It can start in birds.
Then it can migrate to people.
It can become an epidemic.
The epidemic can be "bird flu."

Revision Decisions: Talking Through Sentences and Beyond by Jeff Anderson and Deborah Dean. Copyright © 2014. Stenhouse Publishers.

APPENDIX 9.3   Lesson Set 9: The Collaboration

9.1   Things occurred to Benjamin.
His farm could function even more efficiently.
Putting things on a schedule would be efficient.
He could use the schedule of a clock.
He could schedule the day's waking, hauling, rinsing,
        rolling, and baking on this schedule.

9.2   Clocks weren't common.
Not everybody had one in the 1700s.
This was especially true for regular folks.
Folks such as farmers were regular folks.
But Benjamin's way of approaching the world was far
        from regular.

9.3   (Try starting with *Though*.)
He had never seen a timepiece.
He didn't know how a clock worked.
He set out to build one.
He would be using wood pieces
The pieces were from Stout's timber shed.

9.4   He borrowed a watch.
The watch was a pocket watch.
He studied its innards.
He got to work.

9.5   The man was math-happy.
He drew plans for clocks.
He carved cogs.
He fashioned the clock's face.
He fashioned the hands of the clock.
He added a bell.

Revision Decisions: Talking Through Sentences and Beyond by Jeff Anderson and Deborah Dean. Copyright © 2014. Stenhouse Publishers.

APPENDIX Lesson Set 9: Excerpt from Andrea Pinkney's *Hand in Hand: Ten Black Men Who Changed America* (2012).

It occurred to Benjamin that his farm could function even more efficiently by putting the day's waking, hauling, rinsing, rolling, and baking on a clock's schedule. Clocks weren't common in the 1700s, especially for regular folk such as farmers. But Benjamin's way of approaching the world was far from regular. Though he had never seen a timepiece and didn't know how a clock worked, he set out to build one using wood pieces from Stout's timber shed. He borrowed a pocket watch, studied its innards, and got to work. The math-happy man drew clock plans, carved cogs, fashioned the clock's face and hands, and added a bell.

Revision Decisions: Talking Through Sentences and Beyond by Jeff Anderson and Deborah Dean. Copyright © 2014. Stenhouse Publishers.

APPENDIX 10.1 Lesson Set 10: The Context

Bugs have affected the outcome of nearly every war ever fought, because bugs carry diseases, including typhus, plague, cholera, yellow fever, malaria, typhoid, and dysentery.

Because bugs carry diseases, including typhus, plague, cholera, yellow fever, malaria, typhoid, and dysentery, **bugs have affected the outcome of nearly every war ever fought**.

Excerpt from Sarah Albee's *Bugged: How Insects Changed History* (2014).

Revision Decisions: Talking Through Sentences and Beyond by Jeff Anderson and Deborah Dean. Copyright © 2014. Stenhouse Publishers.

APPENDIX Lesson Set 10: The Practice

Something happened for many years.

They attacked ships.

They looted ships.

The ships sailed off the coast.

The coast was by their settlement.

The settlement was called the Barbary States.

Revision Decisions: Talking Through Sentences and Beyond by Jeff Anderson and Deborah Dean. Copyright © 2014. Stenhouse Publishers.

APPENDIX 10.3   Lesson Set 10: The Collaboration

10.1   These people were known.
       They were known as the Barbary Pirates.
       The Barbary Pirates were famous.

10.2   Something happened five hundred years ago.
       Spain discovered fine goods and treasures.
       The fine goods and treasures were of the New World.
       Pirates became a danger.
       They became a special danger.

10.3   The news spread among the pirates.
       The news was of Spanish treasure ships.
       The ships were carrying emeralds.
       The ships were carrying gold.
       The ships were carrying silver.
       The ships were carrying pearls.
       The ships were carrying other cargo.
       The ships were carrying these treasures back to
          Europe.

10.4   The Spanish traders sailed ships.
       The ships were large.
       The ships were armed.
       The ships were called galleons.

10.5   The pirates watched for the galleons.
       They watched for returning galleons.
       They especially watched for ships coming from major
          trading ports.
       The major trading ports were Havana, Cartagena,
          and Porto Bello.

Revision Decisions: Talking Through Sentences and Beyond by Jeff Anderson and Deborah Dean. Copyright © 2014. Stenhouse Publishers.

APPENDIX 10.4 Lesson Set 10: Excerpt from Gail Gibbons's *Pirates: Robbers of the High Seas* (1993).

Around 1300, bands of ruthless pirates set up settlements along the North African coast. For many years they attacked and looted ships that sailed off the coast of their settlement, the Barbary States. These people were known as the famous Barbary pirates. About five hundred years ago, when Spain discovered the fine goods and treasures of the New World, pirates became a special danger. The news of Spanish treasure ships carrying emeralds, gold, silver, pearls, and other cargo back to Europe spread among the pirates. The Spanish traders sailed large armed ships called galleons. The pirates watched for the returning galleons, especially those coming from the major trading ports of Havana, Cartagena, and Porto Bello.

Revision Decisions: Talking Through Sentences and Beyond by Jeff Anderson and Deborah Dean. Copyright © 2014. Stenhouse Publishers.

REFERENCES

Professional Resources

Anderson, Jeff. 2005. *Mechanically Inclined: Building Grammar, Usage, and Style into Writer's Workshop.* Portland, ME: Stenhouse.

———. 2007. *Everyday Editing: Inviting Students to Use Craft and Skill in Writer's Workshop.* Portland, ME: Stenhouse.

———. 2011. *10 Things Every Writer Needs to Know.* Portland, ME: Stenhouse.

Braddock, Richard Reed, Richard Lloyd-Jones, and Lowell A. Schoer. 1963. *Research in Written Composition.* Urbana, IL: NCTE.

Britton, James. 1993. *Language and Learning: The Importance of Speech in Learning Development.* Portsmouth, NH: Heinemann.

Christensen, Francis. 2007. *Notes Toward a New Rhetoric.* Booklocker.com (Reprint). http://assets.booklocker.com/pdfs/3213s.pdf.

Clark, Peter Roy. 2013. "The Short Sentence as Gospel Truth." Sept. 7, 2013 http://opinionator.blogs.nytimes.com/2013/09/07/the-short-sentence-as-gospel-truth/?_r=0.

Connors, Robert J. 2000. "The Erasure of the Sentence." *CCC* 52 (1): 96–128.

Dean, Deborah. 2010. *What Works in Writing Instruction.* Urbana, IL: NCTE.

Eagleman, David. 2011. *Incognito: The Secret Lives of the Brain.* New York: Pantheon.

Garner, Betty K. 2007. *Getting to Got It! Helping Struggling Students Learn How to Learn.* Alexandria, VA: ASCD.

Graham, Steve, and Dolores Perin. 2007. *Writing Next: Effective Strategies to Improve Writing of Adolescents in Middle and High Schools.* Washington, DC: Alliance for Excellent Education.

Hart, Jack. 2006. *A Writer's Coach.* New York: Pantheon.

Langer, Judith, Elizabeth Close, Janet Angelis, and Paula Preller. 2000. *Guidelines for Teaching Middle and High School Students to Read and Write Well: Six Features of Effective Instruction.* Albany, NY: National Research Center on English Learning and Achievement.

Lehrer, Jonah. 2010. *How We Decide.* New York: Mariner.

Macrorie, Ken. 1988. *The I-Search Paper.* Portsmouth, NH: Boynton/Cook.

Marzano, Robert, Debra Pickering, and Jane E. Pollock. 2007. *Classroom Instruction That Works: Research-Based Strategies for Increasing Student Achievement.* Alexandria, VA: ASCD.

Murray, Donald M. 1990. *Shoptalk*. Portsmouth, NH: Boynton/Cook.

Myhill, Debra. 2005. "Ways of Knowing: Writing with Grammar in Mind." *English Teaching: Practice and Critique* 4 (3): 77–96.

Nagin, Carl, and National Writing Project. 2006. *Because Writing Matters: Improving Student Writing in Our Schools*. San Francisco: Jossey-Bass.

Noden, Harry R. 2011. *Image Grammar*. 2nd ed. Portsmouth, NH: Boynton/Cook Heinemann.

Ray, Katie Wood. 1999. *Wondrous Words: Writers and Writing in the Elementary Classroom*. Urbana, IL: NCTE.

———. 2006. "Exploring Inquiry as a Teaching Stance in the Writing Workshop." *Language Arts* 83 (3): 238–47.

Schuster, Edgar. 2005. "Sentence Comparison: An Activity for Teaching Style." *English Journal* 94 (5): 94–98.

Tovani, Cris. 2000. *I Read It but I Don't Get It: Comprehension Strategies for Adolescent Readers*. Portland, ME: Stenhouse.

Tufte, Virginia. 2006. *Artful Sentences: Syntax as Style*. Cheshire, CT: Graphics Press.

Yagoda, Ben. 2004. "Style: A Pleasure for the Reader, or the Writer?" *Chronicle of Higher Education* 50 (49): B16.

Literature

Albee, Sarah. 2014. *Bugged: How Insects Changed History*. New York: Bloomsbury.

Anderson, Laurie Halse. 2008. *Chains*. New York: Scholastic.

Arnosky, Jim. 2008. *Wild Tracks! A Guide to Nature's Footprints*. New York: Sterling.

———. 2012. *Creep and Flutter: The Secret World of Insects and Spiders*. New York: Sterling.

Berne, Jennifer. 2013. *On a Beam of Light: A Story of Albert Einstein*. San Francisco: Chronicle.

Brooks, Max. 2003. *The Zombie Survival Guide: Complete Protection from the Living Dead*. New York: Three Rivers.

Burleigh, Robert. 2004. *Seurat and La Grande Jatte: Connecting the Dots*. New York: Harry N. Abrams.

Burns, Loree Griffin. 2007. *Tracking Trash: Flotsam, Jetsam, and the Science of Ocean Motion*. Boston: Houghton Mifflin.

Collard, Sneed B, III. 2012. *Most Fun Book Ever About Lizards*. Watertown, MA: Charlesbridge.

Collins, Suzanne. 2010. *The Hunger Games*. New York: Scholastic.

Davies, Nicola. 2009. *What's Eating You? Parasites—The Inside Story*. Somerville, MA: Candlewick.

Fox, Mem. 1988. *Guess What?* Orlando, FL: Omnibus.

Gaiman, Neil. 2013. *Fortunately, the Milk*. New York: Harper Collins.

George-Warren, Holly. 2001. *Shake, Rattle & Roll: The Founders of Rock and Roll*. Boston: Houghton Mifflin.

Gerwitz, Adina Rishe. 2013. *Zebra Forest*. Somerville, MA: Candlewick.

Gibbons, Gail. 1993. *Pirates: Robbers of the High Seas*. New York: Little, Brown.

Giovanni, Nikki. 2005. *Rosa*. New York: Scholastic.

Gladwell, Malcolm. 2011. *Outliers: The Story of Success*. New York: Back Bay.

———. 2013. *David and Goliath: Underdogs, Misfits, and the Art of Battling Giants*. New York: Little, Brown.

Harkrader, L. D. 2008. *Airball: My Life in Briefs*. New York: Square Fish.

Heiligman, Deborah. 2009. *Charles and Emma: The Darwins' Leap of Faith*. New York: Henry Holt.

Hemingway, Ernest. 1964. *A Moveable Feast*. New York: Charles Scribner's Sons.

Hillenbrand, Laura. 2001. *Seabiscuit: An American Legend*. New York: Ballantine.

———. 2010. *Unbroken: A World War II Story of Survival, Resilience, and Redemption*. New York: Random House.

House, Silas. 2005. *The Coal Tattoo*. New York: Ballantine.

Jenkins, Steve. 1997. *Biggest, Strongest, Fastest*. New York: HMH.

———. 2009a. *Never Smile at a Monkey*. New York: Houghton Mifflin.

———. 2009b. *Down, Down, Down: A Journey to the Bottom of the Sea*. New York: Houghton Mifflin.

———. 2012. *The Beetle Book*. New York: HMH.

Joyce, James. 2012. *Dubliners*. New York: Urban Romantics.

Kurlansky, Mark. 2011. *World Without Fish*. Workman Publishing: New York.

Leedy, Loreen. 1993. *Tracks in the Sand*. New York: Doubleday.

Mann, Charles C. 2009. *Before Columbus: The Americas of 1491*. New York: Holt McDougal.

Marrin, Albert. 2006. *Oh, Rats! The Story of Rats and People*. New York: Dutton.

———. 2011. *Flesh and Blood So Cheap: The Triangle Fire and Its Legacy*. New York: Knopf for Young Readers.

———. 2012. *Black Gold: The Story of Oil in Our Lives*. New York: Knopf for Young Readers.

McGavin, George C. 2002. *Smithsonian Handbooks: Insects*. London: DK.

Miller, Heather Lynn. 2008. *This Is Your Life Cycle*. New York: Clarion.

Moss, Michael. 2013. *Salt, Sugar, and Fat: How the Food Giants Hooked Us*. New York: Random House.

Ness, Patrick. 2013. *A Monster Calls*. Somerville, MA. Candlewick.

Pinkney, Andrea. 2012. *Hand in Hand: Ten Black Men Who Changed America*. New York: Disney Hyperion.

Rawls, Wilson. 1961. *Where the Red Fern Grows*. New York: Bantam.

Roach, Mary. 2013. *Gulp: Adventures on the Alimentary Canal*. New York: W. W. Norton.

Sayre, April Pulley. 2013. *Here Come the Humpbacks!* Watertown, MA: Charlesbridge.

Seuss, Dr. 1948. *Thidwick the Big-Hearted Moose*. New York: Random House.

Sheinkin, Steve. 2009. *Two Miserable Presidents: The Amazing, Terrible, and Totally True Story of the Civil War*. New York: Square Fish.

———. 2010. *Which Way to the Wild West? Everything Your Schoolbooks Didn't Tell You About Westward Expansion*. New York: Square Fish.

———. 2012. *Bomb: The Race to Build—and Steal—the World's Most Dangerous Weapon*. New York: Flash Point.

———. 2014. *The Port Chicago 50: Disaster, Mutiny, and The Fight for Civil Rights*. New York: Roaring Book Press.

Snyder, Laurel. 2011. *Bigger Than a Bread Box*. New York: Yearling.

Stead, Rebecca. 2013. *Liar & Spy*. New York: Yearling.

Thompson, Neal. 2013. *A Curious Man: The Strange and Brilliant Life of Robert "Believe It or Not!" Ripley*. New York: Crown Archetype.

Turnage, Sheila. 2012. *Three Times Lucky*. New York: Dial.

Urban, Linda. 2007. *A Crooked Kind of Perfect*. New York: Houghton Mifflin.

Walker, Sally M. 2011. *Blizzard of Glass: The Halifax Explosion of 1917*. New York: Scholastic.

Ward, Helen. 2001. *The Tin Forest*. New York: Puffin.

Zusak, Markus. 2007. *The Book Thief*. New York: Alfred A. Knopf.

INDEX

Page numbers followed by an *f* indicate figures.